FAVORITE RECIPES

A SEVENTY-YEAR COLLECTION

BY JUANITA HOWARD

Grammy's Favorite Recipes: A Seventy Year Collection

Cover Design and Interior Layout by Bradley S. Cobb

Printed in the USA by CreateSpace.

ISBN: 1512129879
ISBN-13: 978-1512129878

OCTOGENERIAN:

The dictionary tells us that word refers to a person in their eighties. But what does it mean to the person whom it is describing? It means many decades of living, living in myriad places and situations. It means a lot of years' worth of experience and a storehouse of memories; most of which are fondly recalled.

In my case, it refers to a girl who grew up on a farm in Muskogee County; co-existing with seven other siblings and a hard working mother and dad. It meant a lot of cold mornings, milking cows by lantern in a cold and dark barn. It meant getting home on the bus after school to tend to the chores that awaited; feeding chickens and gathering eggs, feeding the hogs, to say nothing of hoeing corn and chopping cotton in season, all in preparation for helping with the harvest. It also meant canning fruits and vegetables in a hot kitchen every summer.

There were four boys and four girls so the work was divided according to age and gender. We girls did most of the inside chores while the boys helped Daddy with the outside chores.

It means decades of family get-togethers, the joy we shared at our picnics, the happy gatherings of family reunions and the shared sorrow at funerals as we said good bye to a loved one.

It meant regular attendance at the church in nearby Boynton on Sunday and Wednesday night. It meant learning to help in whatever need might arise. Being reared in the depression era, 'make do' was an often-used expression.

One of the primary needs of a large family is meal preparation. It was a given that, along with all the other requirements of country living, the girls learned to cook meals at an early age. Out of this necessity, for this octogenarian, grew a love for planning, cooking and serving meals for family and friends. With two older sisters, four younger brothers and a younger sister, meals in those early days were a project.

Older sisters Evelyn and Eunice and brother Joe have passed beyond the vale of this life. Brothers John, Jerry and Jim, and Sister Margaret and I, along with our families, still have a reunion each year to relive memories and share our lives.

This book will contain recipes that have been gathered for over seventy years. There is no claim of originality. They come from Mothers, Grandmothers, Sisters, Children, Grandchildren and friends. They are the product of sharing and searching and are garnered from many, many sources. If there is any originality, it will be those to which I have added, deleted, tweaked and otherwise altered to suit the needs and desires of those for whom I have cooked through all these years.

Table of Contents

APPETIZERS, DIPS, and SNACKS

SALADS

SALAD DRESSINGS and SAUCES

SANDWICHES

SOUPS

VEGETABLES and CASSEROLES

BREAKFAST

BEEF

CHICKEN

PORK

SEAFOOD & FISH

DESSERTS

CAKES

PIES and PIE CRUSTS

COBBLERS

COOKIES

CANDY

BREADS

MISCELLANEOUS

APPETIZERS,
DIPS,
and SNACKS

HUMMUS

- 2 16 oz. cans garbanzo beans
- 1 T. Olive Oil
- ¼ c. fresh lemon juice
- 1 clove of garlic
- 1 t. cumin

Blend together in blender. Season with salt after blending. Serve with veggies or chips.

EUNICE'S DIP

- 1 16 oz. can chili with beans
- 4 green onions, chopped
- 1 lb. Velveeta cheese
- 4 oz. can chopped green chilies

Heat and serve with chips

This recipe is from my sister, Eunice.

SHRIMP DIP

- 1 8 oz. package cream cheese
- 1 8 oz. container sour cream
- ½ c. chopped onion
- ½ c. chopped celery
- 2 small cans shrimp

Season with salt, pepper and garlic salt. Serve with chips, crackers or veggies.

CONNIE'S BEAN DIP

- 1 29 oz. can refried beans
- 1 4 oz. can diced green chilies
- 1½ c. grated cheddar cheese
- 1 16 oz. jar mild green chili salsa

Stir all ingredients together and heat in sauce pan, fondue pot, crock-pot or microwave. Serve hot with Doritos or other type of corn chips.

This recipe is from my sister-in-law, Connie Norwood.

DIP FOR FRESH FRUIT

- 1 can sweetened condensed milk
- 1 8 oz. carton sour cream
- ¼ c. fresh lemon juice
- 1 t. vanilla
- Almond flavoring (opt.)

Mix all ingredients together; it will be a little thin, but it will thicken. Put in refrigerator for several hours. Serve with fresh fruit.

This is my daughter Carolyn's recipe.

CHILI CHEESE DIP

- 1 lb. Colby Jack cheese, cubed
- 1 lb. Cheddar cheese, cubed
- 1 16 oz. can chili without beans
- 4 green onions, chopped
- 1 4 oz. can diced green chilies

Mix all in a crock pot. Cook on low for 2 to 4 hours. Serve with tortilla chips.

MARY'S DIP

- 1 16 oz. container sour cream
- 1 pkg. Good Seasons Dressing mix

Mix and serve with chips or veggies.

My friend Mary Bryant and I worked together for about 10 years.

CALIFORNIA DIP

- 1 pkg. Lipton Onion Soup
- 8 oz. container sour cream
- 8 oz. cream cheese (softened)

Mix soup with ½ c. water and heat stirring constantly until onions plump and mixture thickens. Mix with cream cheese until well blended then add sour cream and blend. Serve with chips.

CHICKEN CRUMPETS

- 4 5 oz. cans boned chicken
- 1 8 oz. package cream cheese
- ½ onion, minced
- ½ green pepper, minced

Trim slices of white bread and brush each slice of trimmed bread with melted butter. Put some of the mixture on each slice of bread; bring corners together and hold with a toothpick. Heat in 350 degree oven until hot and browned.

This recipe is from a very dear friend Jo June Willis Dipboye.

CHEESE BALL

- 2 8 oz. pkgs. cream cheese
- 1 jar chipped beef
- 1 bunch of green onions, chopped
- ½ t. garlic powder

Mix well and form into a ball.

OYSTER CRACKERS

- 1 pkg. oyster crackers
- 1 pkg. original ranch style dressing
- ½ t. garlic salt
- ½ t. dill weed
- 1 t. lemon pepper
- ¾ c. oil, heated

Put crackers in a bowl that has a lid. Sprinkle next 4 ingredients over crackers. Pour the hot oil over the crackers with seasonings; cover and shake. Do not shake until the hot oil has been added.

This is another recipe from Eunice.

COCKTAIL SAUSAGE

- 2 lbs. sausage
- ½ c. bread crumbs
- 2 eggs

Mix well and form small balls. Brown and drain well. Put in oven and baste with orange cranberry sauce. 325 degree oven – 30 minutes.

SCRABBLE

- 1 box pretzel thins
- 1 box Cheerios

- 1 box each: rice Chex and wheat Chex
- 2 lbs. salted mixed nuts
- 2 c. salad oil
- 2 T. Worcestershire sauce
- 1 T. garlic salt
- 1 T. seasoned salt

Put salad oil and seasonings together then pour over the other ingredients which have been mixed and put into a large roaster pan. Cook in a 250 degree oven for 2 hours, stirring every 30 minutes.

Another recipe from Sister Eunice, but all of my siblings make this recipe, especially at Christmas.

GUACAMOLE

- 1 medium tomato, peeled and diced
- ½ small onion, minced
- 2 medium avocados, mashed with 2 T. fresh lemon juice
- 1¼ t. salt
- 1 small garlic clove, minced
- 1 4 oz. can chopped mild green chilies, drained

Mix well.

MARINATED MUSHROOMS

- 2 lbs. fresh mushrooms
- ½ t. cumin seed
- 1 large bottle or jar Italian dressing
- 4 green onions, chopped

Remove stems and lightly wash mushrooms and drain on a paper towel. Leave mushrooms whole. Mix in all other ingredients. Marinate at room temperature for six hours.

ORANGE CRANBERRY SAUCE

- 1 16 oz. can whole cranberry sauce
- ¼ c. orange juice
- 3 T. honey

MOM'S DEVILED EGGS

- 1 dz. eggs
- Salt and pepper to taste
- 3 T. mayonnaise
- 2 t. catsup
- ½ t. vinegar
- 3 T. sweet pickle juice
- 1½ t. mustard

Boil eggs, cool and cut in half. Remove yolks and mix with other ingredients. Fill egg whites with mixture. Top with paprika.

PERFECT BOILED EGGS

Put eggs in a large heavy pot and cover with cold water. Bring to a boil and boil 10 minutes. Remove from heat; drain and cover with cold water until cooled.

CRAB APPETIZERS

- ½ c. butter
- 1½ t. garlic salt
- 1 6 oz. jar Old English Cheese Spread
- 1 7 oz. can crabmeat
- 1½ t. mayonnaise
- 6 English muffins (split)

Blend first 5 ingredients and spread on muffins. Freeze on a cookie sheet until hard. Cut into quarters and keep frozen until ready to use. Brown muffins under the broiler for a few minutes at serving time. Makes 48.

This recipe is from my sister, Evelyn Schunk.

PATTY'S SALSA DIP

- 1 29 oz. can tomatoes
- 1 onion, chopped
- 3 to 4 jalapeno peppers, chopped
- 1 T. cumin
- 1 T. Accent
- 1 T. garlic powder
- 1 T. black pepper
- 1 T. sugar
- 2 T. oil
- 1 can Rotel tomatoes

Mix together and put in pan. Bring to a boil; lower heat and simmer for 30 minutes. Can be served hot or cold with chips.

This recipe is from Patty Boulter, a long time best friend of my daughter, Carolyn.

LAYERED MEXICAN DIP

Layer in following order in a 12 X 8 inch pan or dish:

- 1 16 oz. can refried beans mixed with ½ package of taco seasoning mix
- 1 pkg. frozen avocado dip, thawed
- 1 8 oz. carton sour cream
- 1 4½ oz. can chopped black olives
- 2 large tomatoes, chopped

- 1 small onion, chopped
- 1 4 oz. can chopped green chilies
- 1½ c. Jack cheese, shredded

Serve with tortilla chips.

ROASTED NUTS

Toss:

- 1 c. almonds
- 1 c. walnuts
- 1 c. pecans
- 3 T. olive oil
- 2 t. Worcestershire sauce
- 4 sprigs of fresh thyme or rosemary
- a pinch of red pepper flakes
- sea salt
- pepper.

Roast in the oven at 350 degrees on a baking sheet for 20 to 25 minutes.

Nuts are full of fiber and can help keep your blood sugar levels stable and lower your risk of type 2 diabetes.

DILL DIP

- 1 c. mayonnaise
- 3 T. grated onion
- 1 c. sour cream
- 1 T. dill weed
- 1 T. parsley
- 1 ½ t. seasoned salt

Mix ingredients and chill.

STUFFED JALAPENOS

Clean, seed, and half Jalapenos. (Be careful as they can burn your hands. I wear gloves.)

Brown 1 lb. sausage and add:

- l bag bacon bits
- 1 ½ c. shredded Jack cheese
- 2 8 oz. pkgs. cream cheese
- 3 or 4 chopped green onions.

Mix well. Stuff peppers and bake at 325 degrees until bubbly.

This recipe is from one of my favorite nieces, Vickie McDaniel Tracy. She brought these to our last family reunion, and they disappeared very quickly.

SALADS

GREEN BEAN SALAD

- 1 can green beans
- 1 can yellow wax beans
- 1 can red kidney beans

Drain; place in bowl and add:

- ½ c. minced green pepper
- ½ c. minced onion

Mix the following together and pour over the salad:

- ½ c. salad oil
- ½ c. vinegar
- ¾ c. sugar
- 1 t. salt
- ½ t. black pepper

Refrigerate overnight.

Eunice's recipe.

ROMAINE SALAD

- Romaine lettuce
- Apple chopped and unpeeled
- Raisins
- Bleu Cheese

Layer and drizzle with Poppy Seed dressing.

PASTA SALAD

- 1 small pkg. spaghetti, cooked
- 1 large jar sliced mushrooms
- 1 bunch broccoli tops, chopped
- 2 small tomatoes, chopped
- 2 bunches green onions, chopped
- 2 bottles Italian dressing

Mix and marinate overnight. The spaghetti will absorb all the dressing.

Another recipe from my sister, Evelyn.

ELIZABETH SALAD

- 1 pkg. lime Jell-O
- 1 pkg. lemon Jell-O
- ½ c. hot water
- 1 c. crushed pineapple, drained
- 1½ c. sour cream
- ½ c. milk
- 1 c. cottage cheese

Dissolve Jell-O in hot water. Cool. Fold in 1 c. sour cream, milk, cottage cheese and pineapple. Pour into lightly greased mold and chill. Top with remaining sour cream.

Eunice's recipe.

POTATO SALAD

- 8 boiled and diced new potatoes
- ½ diced purple onion
- 1 grated carrot
- 3 heaping T. mayonnaise
- 4 boiled and grated eggs
- 3 dill pickles, grated
- 1 stalk celery, diced
- 1 heaping T. mustard
- Salt and pepper to taste.

Mix well.

This recipe is from Maudie Brewer, a lady with whom I worked.

CHERRY COLA SALAD

- 1 can bing cherries
- 1 1/3 c. crushed pineapple
- 1 (12 oz.) cola
- 2 pkgs. black cherry Jell-O
- ½ c. pecans, chopped

Drain fruit juice and add water to make 2 cups. Heat and pour over Jell-O. Cool and add fruit, cola and nuts. Chill.

This is a recipe from Ruth Wimberly, a very dear friend with whom I lived for one year prior to my marriage to my husband, Bill.

BROCCOLI SALAD

- 1 bunch broccoli, chopped
- 10 to 12 slices bacon, crumbled
- 1 medium red onion, chopped
- 1 c. cheddar cheese, grated

Dressing:

- 1 c. mayonnaise
- ½ c. sugar
- 3 T. vinegar

Mix dressing ingredients and toss with salad.

This recipe is from Barbara Postal of our Ladies Bible Class.

GRAPE SALAD

Vanilla yogurt. Mix with grapes cut in half. Sprinkle with powdered sugar and mix again.

Topping:

Sprinkle with brown sugar and chopped pecans.

CRANBERRY SALAD (1)

- 1 lb. cranberries, chopped
- 1½ c. sugar
- 1 c. Tokay grapes
- 1 c. miniature marshmallows
- ½ c. chopped nuts
- 1 c. whipping cream, whipped

Mix cranberries and sugar and store in refrigerator overnight. Cut up Tokay grapes and store in refrigerator overnight. Just before serving, mix the grapes with cranberries and sugar, then add marshmallows and chopped nuts. Fold in freshly whipped cream.

CRANBERRY SALAD (2)

- 1 16 oz. can crushed pineapple
- 1 c. water
- 2 pkgs. (3 oz. each) strawberry or raspberry gelatin
- 1 16 oz. can cranberry sauce (either whole or jellied)
- ½ c. nuts, chopped
- ½ c. celery, finely chopped
- 1 12 oz. can Coke

In large saucepan, mix crushed pineapple and water. Bring to boil. Add dry gelatin and cranberry sauce. Mix well and stir in remaining ingredients. Refrigerate until jelled.

CRANBERRY SALAD (3)

- 1 lb. cranberries
- 2 c. sugar

Cook until berries pop open.

- 2 pkgs. cherry Jell-O
- 2 c. hot water

Mix together Jell-O and water and stir into cranberry mixture.

Add the following to the above mixture and refrigerate until set:

- 2 apples, diced
- 2 oranges, diced
- 3 stalks celery, chopped
- 1 c. pecans, chopped
- 1 15 oz. can crushed pineapple

FRUIT SALAD (1)

- 1 20 oz. can sliced peaches, drained and reserve juice
- 1 20 oz. can sliced pears, drained
- 1 20 oz. can crushed pineapple, drained
- 2 bananas, sliced horizontally
- ½ c. strawberries, sliced

1 small pkg. instant vanilla pudding mix

Mix all fruit in a large bowl. Pour dry pudding mix over and stir gently. If needed, add some of the reserved peach juice. Refrigerate overnight. Serves 10 to 12.

FRUIT SALAD (2)

- 1 8 oz. pkg. cream cheese
- 1 14 oz. can sweetened condensed milk
- 1 3.4 oz. box instant lemon pudding mix
- 1 15 oz. can sliced peaches, drained
- 1 15 oz. can sliced pears, drained
- 1 15 oz. can crushed pineapple, drained
- 1 15 oz. can mandarin oranges, drained

In large bowl of electric mixer, combine cream cheese, sweetened condensed milk and pudding mix. Beat about 2 minutes. Remove from mixer and gently stir in peaches, pears, oranges and pineapple. Cover and refrigerate overnight.

SPINACH SALAD

- Baby spinach leaves
- Candied walnuts*
- Feta cheese crumbles
- Pears, peeled and sliced

Toss all ingredients with Marzetti's sweet oil and vinegar dressing.

*Place chopped walnuts in pan over medium heat. Cover with sugar. Stir until sugar melts and covers walnuts. Spread over waxed paper to cool and dry.

This recipe is from one of my favorite granddaughters, Lauren Perkins Walker.

CRAB SALAD

- 2 small pkgs. spiral macaroni, cooked
- 2 lbs. crab meat
- 1 bell pepper, diced
- 1 onion, diced
- 8 oz. cheddar cheese, cubed
- Miracle Whip or Italian Dressing to suit taste

Mix well. Serve with crackers.

Another recipe from Patty Boulter.

MARINATED CUCUMBERS AND ONIONS

- 1 c. ice cubes
- 1/3 c. water
- ¾ c. white distilled vinegar
- 3 T. sugar
- 2 t. basil
- ¾ t. salt

Put all above ingredients into a glass bowl and stir until sugar is dissolved. Add a thinly sliced small red onion and medium cucumber. Refrigerate until ready to serve. Remove with slotted spoon and arrange on lettuce with 2 tomatoes, cut into wedges. Serves 4.

TABOULI SALAD

- 16 oz. cracked bulgur wheat
- 4 t. salt
- 2 t. pepper
- 1½ c. lemon juice
- 1½ c. oil
- 1 bunch parsley, chopped
- 1 bunch green onions, chopped
- 1 large bell pepper, diced
- 1 cucumber, diced
- 4 tomatoes, diced

Mix bulgur wheat, salt, pepper, lemon juice and oil. Add parsley, green onions, bell pepper, cucumber and tomatoes. Chill at least one hour.

MARY'S LAYERED SALAD

Layer in order:

- 1 head lettuce, torn into pieces
- 1 bag spinach, torn into pieces
- 1 bunch green onions, chopped
- 1 10 oz. pkg. frozen peas, thawed and uncooked
- 1 lb. crisp bacon, crumbled
- 6 boiled eggs, sliced

Dressing:

- 1 pkg. original Hidden Valley Ranch Style Dressing
- 1 c. sour cream
- 1 c. mayonnaise

Mix dressing and spread over top of layers. Refrigerate overnight.

This is another of Mary Bryant's recipes.

CUCUMBER AND ONIONS IN VINEGAR

- 1 c. white vinegar
- ¾ c. sugar
- ¾ c. water
- 1 t. salt
- 1/8 t. black pepper
- 1/8 t. red pepper (opt)
- 1/8 t. basil (opt)
- 1 large onion, peeled and sliced
- 3 cucumbers, peeled and sliced

In a sauce pan heat vinegar, sugar and water, stirring until sugar is dissolved. Add salt, peppers and basil. Set aside to cool. Cover onions and cucumbers with cooled liquid. Cover and refrigerate at least 2 to 4 hours before serving.

CHICKEN SALAD (1)

- 4 c. cooked and seasoned cubed chicken
- 1 c. celery, chopped
- 1 c. crushed pineapple with a little juice
- 1 c. mayonnaise
- ½ c. pecans
- 1½ T. Lemon Pepper

Mix and serve. This makes a nice luncheon served on leaf lettuce with hot rolls and green peas.

CHICKEN SALAD WITH GRAPES

- 3 c. cooked chicken, diced
- 1½ c. celery, diced
- 3 T. lemon juice
- 1½ c. seedless green grapes
- ¾ c. slivered almonds, toasted

Dressing:

- 1 c. mayonnaise
- ¼ c. light cream
- 1½ t. salt
- 1 t. dry mustard
- Pepper to taste

Combine chicken, celery and lemon juice and chill at least 1 hour. Then add grapes and almonds. Mix ingredients for the dressing and combine with chicken mixture. Serves 8 to 10.

CHICKEN SALAD (2)

- ¾ c. mayonnaise
- 1 T. onion, finely chopped
- 3 c. cubed cooked chicken
- 2 T. sour cream
- ½ t. curry powder
- ½ c. celery, diced

Combine mayonnaise, sour cream, onion, curry powder with ¼ t. salt and a dash of pepper. Stir in chicken and celery. Cover and chill. Make sandwiches or serve on lettuce.

ORANGE SALAD

- 1 large box orange gelatin
- 1 large container cottage cheese
- 1 can mandarin oranges, drained
- 1 can chunk pineapple, drained
- 1 9 oz. container of cool whip
- 1 c. miniature marshmallows (opt)

Blend dry gelatin and cottage cheese until smooth and not grainy. Add fruit. Fold in cool whip and marshmallows. Refrigerate. Makes a large salad.

BLUEBERRY JELL-O SALAD

- 1 large pkg. raspberry Jell-O
- 2 c. hot water

Dissolve Jell-O in water and add:

- 1 can crushed pineapple, drained
- 1 can blueberry pie filling

Put in refrigerator until set. Then beat together

- 8 oz. cream cheese
- 1 c. sour cream
- ¾ c. sugar

Spread over set Jell-O.

This recipe is from Sharon Childers of our Ladies Bible Class.

GOLDIE'S COLESLAW

- 8 c. shredded fine cabbage
- 1/8 t. garlic powder
- 2 T. sugar
- 1 t. salt
- 1/8 t. pepper
- ¾ c. mayonnaise

Mix all together and refrigerate several hours or overnight. This coleslaw is from Goldie's in Tulsa.

CAULIFLOWER SALAD

- 1 head cauliflower
- ¾ c. mayonnaise
- ½ c. sliced stuffed pimiento olives
- 1½ T. onions, minced

Into a large mixing bowl, slice each section of cauliflower in very thin slices. In a small bowl, mix mayonnaise with olives and onions. Stir into cauliflower. Add salt and pepper to taste. Mix well. Cover and refrigerate overnight. It should serve 10 or 12.

24 HOUR SALAD

- 3 egg yolks
- 1 c. heavy cream, whipped
- 2 T. sugar
- Dash of salt
- 2 c. pitted white cherries
- 2 T. vinegar
- 2 T. pineapple syrup
- 2 c. quartered marshmallows
- 2 c. pineapple tidbits
- 2 oranges, cut into pieces
- 1 T. butter

Cook egg yolks, sugar, salt, vinegar, pineapple syrup and butter in double boiler until thick. Cool. Fold in whipped cream, cherries, marshmallows, pineapple and oranges. Chill 24 hours.

This recipe is from Aunt Pearl, my Daddy's sister.

CLASSIC CAPRESE SALAD

- 3 large ripe heirloom tomatoes
- 2 4 oz. fresh mozzarella balls
- Fresh basil leaves
- 2 T. balsamic vinegar
- 2 T fruity extra-virgin olive oil
- ½ t. coarse salt
- ½ t. cracked black pepper

Slice tomatoes into ¼ in. thick rounds. Drain mozzarella from package brine solution and pat dry with a paper towel. Slice into ¼ inch thick rounds. (To make slicing easier, dip your knife into hot water to warm the blade between cuts.) Arrange alternating slices of tomato and mozzarella and basil leaves on four plates. Drizzle with balsamic vinegar and olive oil, sprinkle with salt and pepper and a scattering of torn basil leaves. Set aside 5 minutes to allow flavors to intensify. Serves 4.

SALAD DRESSINGS and SAUCES

WALDORF SALAD SURPRISE DRESSING

- ¾ c. creamy peanut butter
- ¼ c. honey
- ½ c. mayonnaise

Blend ingredients. Serve with Waldorf salad or cabbage and apple salad.

CROUTONS

- 1 14 oz. loaf sourdough bread, sliced
- ½ c. olive oil
- ¼ t. salt
- 5 cloves garlic, crushed

You can cut bread slices in approximately 1 in. cubes, spread on a cookie and set aside, at room temperature, until they are dry and crisp. In a hurry? Preheat oven to 325 degrees. Put cubes in oven until thoroughly dry. Cool and put in large bowl that can be sealed. In cast iron skillet, or any medium skillet, heat oil. Add salt and garlic. Cook over low heat until garlic starts to sizzle. Remove from heat and pour over croutons. Cover and shake until well coated. Remove cover and let cool completely, tossing from time to time to be sure they are all well coated. Store at room temperature. Serve with salads.

LEMON CHAMPAGNE VINAIGRETTE

- ¼ c. champagne vinegar
- 2 t. lemon juice
- 1 t. Dijon mustard
- ½ c. olive oil
- ½ t. salt
- ¼ t. pepper

In a small bowl, whisk vinegar, lemon juice and Dijon mustard. Gradually whisk in the olive oil.

TARTAR SAUCE

- 1 c. mayonnaise
- 2 T. minced parsley
- 1 to 2 T. dill pickle, minced
- 1 to 2 T. onion, minced
- 1 T. bottled capers
- 1 T. pimento-stuffed olive, minced

In a small bowl with fork, stir together all ingredients until well mixed.

SPAGHETTI SAUCE

- 1 lb. lean ground beef
- 2 8 oz. can tomato sauce
- 1 6 oz. can tomato paste
- 2¾ c. water

Brown ground beef in large skillet on medium-high heat. Drain excess fat. Add sauce, paste and water. Stir in the following ingredients:

- 1 T. instant minced onion
- 1 T. parsley flakes
- 1½ t. salt
- 1 T. cornstarch
- ¼ t. minced garlic
- 2 t. green pepper flakes
- 1 t. sugar
- ¾ t. Italian seasoning

Reduce heat and simmer 30 minutes, stirring occasionally.

LEGEND'S POPPYSEED DRESSING

- 1½ c. sugar
- 2 t. salt
- 2 t. dry mustard
- 2/3 c. white vinegar
- 3 t. onion juice (opt)

- 2 c. peanut oil
- 3 T. poppy seeds

Mix sugar, salt, mustard and vinegar. Add onion juice and stir in thoroughly. Add oil slowly while beating constantly until thick. Add poppy seeds and beat until distributed. Keep refrigerated.

SANDWICHES

EGG SALAD SANDWICHES

- 6 hard-boiled eggs, chopped

Mix the following in a medium bowl:

- ¼ c. mayonnaise
- 1 T. lemon juice
- 1 T. yellow mustard
- ¼ t. salt
- ¼ t. pepper

Add:

- chopped eggs
- ½ c. celery, finely chopped
- ¼ c. green onions, thinly sliced

Mix well.

8 slices rustic wheat bread

4 lettuce leaves

Refrigerate coved to blend flavors. Serve on wheat bread with lettuce leaves.

SUSAN'S SANDWICH RECIPE

- 2 pkgs. Hawaiian sweet rolls
- ½ lb. Cajun roast beef
- ½ lb. pastrami
- ½ lb. turkey
- ½ lb. ham
- ½ lb. provolone cheese
- ½ lb. Swiss cheese

Put together sandwiches in any order you want. Place them on a cookie sheet with raised edges or in a large casserole dish. Melt 1 stick of butter, 2 T. spicy brown mustard, 2 T. Worcestershire sauce together. Pour mixture on top of sandwiches. Sprinkle 2 T. onion flakes on top. Bake at 350 degrees for 15-20 minutes or until cheese melts.

This recipe is from one of my favorite granddaughters, Susan Bole Robinson.

ALFALFA SANDWICH

Toast bread and spread with mayonnaise

Add: Bacon, Avocado, Tomato and alfalfa sprouts.

CHILI BURGERS

- 2 lbs. ground beef
- 2/3 T. chili powder
- ½ c. barbeque sauce
- 2 t. salt
- 2 small cans tomato sauce
- 1 t. paprika
- 1 large onion chopped

Brown onion and meat. Put in rest of ingredients and simmer 20 minutes.

TURKEY BURGERS

- 2 c. cooked turkey, chopped or finely ground
- 1 egg, slightly beaten
- ½ c. mayonnaise
- ½ c. celery, diced
- ¼ c. dry bread crumbs (flavored or plain)
- 2 T. onion, finely chopped
- 2 T. blanched almonds, finely chopped (opt.)
- ¼ t. salt
- ¼ t. pepper

Mix together ingredients. Chill. Shape into 6 patties; roll in more bread crumbs. Melt butter in skillet over medium heat. Cook burgers until evenly browned on both sides.

SOUPS

TURKEY SOUP

- 1 turkey frame (the meatier the better)
- 8 c. water
- 1 onion, chopped
- 2 t. salt
- ¼ t. pepper
- 1 t. Worcestershire sauce
- 1 t. dried sage or poultry seasoning
- 1 bay leaf
- 1 16 oz. pkg. frozen corn
- 1 c. sliced celery
- 1 c. sliced carrots
- 1 c. diced potato
- 2 T. snipped parsley

Fit turkey carcass into Dutch oven, breaking carcass if necessary. Add water, onion, salt, pepper, Worcestershire sauce, sage and bay leaf. Cover and simmer 1½ hours. Remove turkey carcass, cut off meat and dice, return to pot and then add corn, celery, carrot, potato and parsley. Cover and simmer 45 minutes or until vegetables are done, stirring now and then. Makes 8 to 10 servings. (A good way to add flavor is to stir in a chicken bouillon cube or two.)

This recipe is from Shareon Norwood, my brother Jim's wife.

WHITE CHICKEN CHILI

- 2 lbs. chicken, boneless and skinless
- 3 cans of great northern beans
- 1 can Rotel
- 1 T. oil
- 1 onion, chopped
- 2 t. garlic, minced
- 4 oz. can chopped green chilies
- 2 t. ground cumin
- 1 t. oregano
- 1½ t. cayenne
- ½ t. salt
- 14 ½ can chicken broth
- 3 c. Colby jack cheese, shredded
- 16 oz. carton sour cream

Boil chicken and shred. Cook onion and spices in oil until transparent. Combine beans and broth, Rotel, onion and chicken in large pot. Cook for an hour. Add cheese and sour cream to pot and stir together. Once cheese is melted; it is done.

CROCK POT VEGETABLE SOUP

- 1 lb. stew meat
- 1 lb. can tomatoes
- 2 carrots, sliced
- 2 stalks celery, sliced
- 2 medium onions, diced
- 2 medium potatoes, diced
- 3 c. water
- 1 t. salt
- 1 t. chili powder
- 2 bay leaves
- 4 peppercorns
- 3 beef bouillon cubes
- 1 pkg. mixed vegetables

Put all ingredients except vegetables in crock pot. Stir well. Cover and cook on low for 12 to 24 hours. (High 4 to 6 hours) Package of frozen vegetables should be added during last 2 hours of cooking. I use frozen sliced okra instead of mixed vegetables.

BEAN CHOWDER

- 1 lb. pinto beans
- 3 T. bacon fat
- 1 lb. ground beef
- 1 #2 can tomatoes
- 1 t. baking soda
- 1½ t. salt
- 1 large onion, chopped
- ½ c. catsup
- 1 pkg. chili seasoning

Cover beans with water. Stir in soda and soak overnight. Drain and wash beans thoroughly to remove soda. Add 1½ cups water, bacon fat and salt. Cover. Simmer beans about 2 hours or until tender. Brown ground beef on medium high heat. Add onion and cook until onion is transparent. Add to beans. Blend tomatoes in blender until smooth and add to beans. Add catsup and chili seasoning. Cover and bring to a boil on medium high heat. Reduce heat and simmer for 45 minutes. Serve piping hot.

This was served in the school cafeteria when my two girls were in grade school. The day they served bean chowder was the only day Janet (daughter #2) would eat in the cafeteria. The other days she would take a peanut butter and jelly sandwich to school for lunch.

CHEESE BROCCOLI SOUP

- ½ c. butter
- 1 onion, chopped
- 1 16 oz. pkg. frozen broccoli
- 4 14.5 oz. cans chicken stock
- 1 lb. Velveeta
- 2 c. milk
- 1 T. garlic powder
- 2/3 c. cornstarch
- 1 c. water

Cook onion in butter until tender but not brown. Stir in broccoli and chicken stock. Simmer. Reduce heat. Add cheese, cut up. Dissolve. Mix in milk and garlic. Dissolve cornstarch in water and slowly add to soup stirring constantly.

This recipe is from Glenna Kuhn, a member of McLoud Writer's Group.

BAKED POTATO SOUP

- 2/3 c. butter or margarine
- 2/3 c. flour
- 7 cups of milk
- 4 large baking potatoes, baked, cooled, peeled and cubed (about 4 cups)
- 4 green onions, sliced
- 12 bacon strips, cooked and crumbled
- 1¼ c. shredded cheddar cheese
- 1 c. sour cream
- ¾ t. salt
- ½ t. pepper

In a large soup kettle or Dutch oven, melt the butter. Stir in flour; heat and stir until smooth. Gradually add milk, stirring constantly until thickened. Add potatoes and onions. Bring to a boil, stirring constantly. Reduce heat; simmer for 10 minutes. Add remaining ingredients; stir until cheese melts. Serve immediately. Yield 8 to 10 servings.

TACO SOUP

- 1 onion, chopped
- 1 can kidney beans
- 2 cans pinto beans
- 1 can corn, drained
- 3 cans stewed tomatoes
- 2 lbs. ground beef
- 1 pkg. taco seasoning mix
- 1 pkg. Hidden Valley Ranch dressing mix (dry)
- 4 oz. can chopped green chilies

Brown beef and onion in a large pot. Season with salt and pepper. Add taco seasoning and mix well. Add Ranch dressing and mix well. Pour canned ingredients into the pot. Simmer stirring occasionally. Serve with shredded cheese, salsa, sour cream, crackers or taco chips.

This recipe is from Virgie Cartner, a long-time good friend.

BLACK-EYED PEA SOUP

- 1 T. olive oil
- 1 large onion, chopped
- 1 clove garlic, minced
- 1 4 oz. can chopped green chilies
- 4 16 oz. cans black-eyed peas, drained and rinsed
- 1 10 oz. can diced tomatoes with green chilies
- 3 11 oz. cans beef broth
- ½ t. salt
- ½ t. pepper
- 6 slices crisp bacon, crumbled

Sauté onion and garlic in olive oil. Add rest of ingredients except bacon and mix well. Cook until heated through. Ladle into soup bowls and sprinkle with bacon.

I like to serve this on New Year's Day. You must eat black-eyed peas on New Year's Day.

VEGETABLES and CASSEROLES

BROCCOLI AND RICE CASSEROLE

- ½ onion, chopped
- ½ c. celery, chopped
- 3 T. oil
- 2 T. butter
- 1 16 oz. pkg. frozen broccoli, cooked and salted
- 1 can cream of chicken soup
- 1 soup can of milk
- 2 c. rice, cooked and salted
- 1 can mushrooms
- 1 small jar Cheez Whiz

Sauté onions and celery in oil. Add butter. Combine soup and milk. Combine all ingredients. Bake in well-greased casserole for 40 minutes at 300 degrees. Cooked chicken bits may be added for a complete meal.

This recipe is from my Aunt Ruby Louise Haninger's cookbook which was written in 1989.

MRS. TOM'S GREEN BEANS

- 2 cans French green beans
- 1 can cream of mushroom soup
- 1 can French-fried onion rings

Boil and drain liquid from beans; add soup. Put into casserole and cover with a can of French fried onion rings. Bake until bubbly in 350 degree oven.

SIMPLE SAUTEED GREENS

- 1½ lbs. fresh spinach
- 2 T. olive oil
- 2 large garlic cloves, minced
- ¼ t. salt
- ½ c. chicken broth

Heat oil in skillet over medium heat. Add garlic; sauté 1 minute. Add spinach, in batches, turning with tongs until wilted. Sprinkle with salt. Add broth and stir to incorporate. Cook, stirring occasionally, 5 to 8 minutes until all of the liquid has evaporated.

FRITO CASSEROLE

- 1 pkg. Fritos
- 2 cans cream of mushroom soup
- 1 lb. cheddar cheese, grated
- 1 can Rotel tomatoes
- 1 onion, chopped

Crumble Fritos into casserole and top with chopped onion and cheese. Mix soup with tomatoes and pour over last. Bake 30 minutes in 350 degree oven.

ZUCCHINI AND TOMATO GRATIN

- 1 T. olive oil
- 2 cloves of garlic, minced
- 2 T. onion, finely chopped
- 2 fresh basil leaves, chopped
- ½ c. minute rice
- 2 small zucchini, sliced ¼ inch thick
- 4 medium tomatoes, sliced ½ inch thick
- 1 c. boiling water
- ½ c. cheddar cheese, grated
- Salt and freshly ground pepper

Preheat oven to 375 degrees. Put the oil in an 8-inch square baking dish and spread to coat the bottom. Sprinkle the garlic, onion and basil over the oil. Spread the rice over the top. Layer the zucchini and tomato slices over the rice and pour the boiling water over the top. Season with salt and pepper. Bake for 20 minutes. Sprinkle the cheese over the top and bake for another 10 to 15 minutes, or until the cheese is golden brown and vegetables and rice are cooked.

SWEET POTATO CASSEROLE

- 3 c. cooked sweet potatoes
- 2/3 c. sugar
- ½ t. salt
- 2 eggs, beaten

- ½ c. milk
- ½ stick butter
- 1 t. vanilla

Topping:

- 1 c. brown sugar
- 1 c. pecans, chopped
- ½ c. flour
- ½ stick butter

Mix sweet potatoes, sugar, salt, eggs, milk, butter and vanilla all together; put in lightly greased casserole dish. For the topping, mix together brown sugar, pecans, flour and butter. Crumble and place on top of potatoes and bake at 350 degrees for 35 minutes.

This is my daughter Carolyn's recipe.

SAVORY BAKED BEANS

- 1 16 to 18 oz. can pork and beans
- 2 T. brown sugar
- ¼ t. dry mustard
- ¼ c. catsup
- 2 slices bacon, cut in 1 inch pieces

Combine ingredients. Bake covered in a greased casserole in 350 degree oven for 20 minutes. Uncover and continue baking for 20 minutes.

SAVORY BAKED LIMAS:

Substitute 3 cups cooked lima beans for the beans in previous recipe.

TWICE BAKED POTATOES

- 2 baking potatoes
- 3 T. butter
- 2 T. onion, grated
- ½ c. cheese, grated
- ½ c. cottage cheese
- 1½ t. salt
- ¼ t. pepper

Preheat oven to 425 degrees. Wash potatoes and pat dry. Rub skins with olive oil and sprinkle with salt and pepper. Prick with a fork in several places. Place on a baking sheet and bake and bake for 50 to 60 minutes, until tender. Let cool slightly. Reduce oven temperature to 350 degrees. Cut each potato in halves lengthwise. Mash pulp and add the rest of ingredients. Beat until fluffy. Pile mix into potato boats; sprinkle with bread crumbs. Dot with butter. Bake for 20 minutes. Serves 4.

ARTICHOKE SWISS STUFFED BAKED POTATOES

- 2 baking potatoes
- 1 6 oz. jar marinated artichokes, chopped with 2 T. of the marinade
- 4 oz. Swiss cheese, shredded

Prepare as directed in the preceding recipe.

BAKED HOMINY GRITS

- 4 c. milk
- ½ c. butter + 1/3 c. butter
- 1 cup grits
- 1 t. salt
- 1/8 t. white pepper
- 1 c. Gruyere cheese (or Jack), grated
- 1/3 c. grated parmesan

Boil milk and add ½ c. butter (cut in pieces). Gradually stir in grits. Boil and stir all the time until done. Season with salt and pepper and beat with an electric mixer for five minutes. Pour into 13 x 9 x 2 casserole and allow to set. Cut in rectangles and pour over 1/3 c. melted butter. Sprinkle with cheeses. Heat oven to 400 degrees and bake for 30 minutes. May be made the day before and baked a little longer if cold.

BROCCOLI CHEESE STUFFED POTATOES

- 2 baking potatoes
- 2/3 c. Alouette or Boursin cheese
- 1½ c. broccoli or cauliflower, microwaved for 2 minutes

Prepare as directed in the preceding recipe.

STEWED OKRA WITH TOMATOES

- 2 T. bacon drippings
- 1 onion, chopped
- 1 green pepper, chopped
- 2 c. fresh tomatoes, chopped
- 2 c. okra, sliced

If fresh tomatoes are not available, canned tomatoes may be used. Heat drippings and add onion, pepper and okra and brown slightly. Add tomatoes, salt and pepper. Cook over moderate heat until okra is tender and the mixture is rather thick, about 20 minutes. Stir to prevent sticking.

This is one of my mother's recipes that she made with fresh vegetables out of her garden.

CORN CASSEROLE

- 1 T. flour
- ¼ c. sugar
- 2 beaten eggs
- ½ stick melted butter
- 1 can whole kernel corn, drained
- 1 can cream style corn

Mix flour and sugar; add eggs. Melt butter and add corn. Bake 40 to 60 minutes in a 350 degree oven.

HOMINY CASSEROLE

- 1 29 oz. cans hominy, drained
- 1 c. sour cream
- 1 t. salt
- 1 lb. Jack cheese, cubed
- 2 cans diced green chilies

Mix all together and bake uncovered in 350 degree oven until hot about 45 minutes.

SQUASH CASSEROLE

- 1 lb. yellow squash
- 1 medium onion, chopped
- ¼ c. butter
- ¼ c. flour
- ½ t. salt
- 1 c. milk
- 1 c. cheddar cheese, grated
- 2 c. green peas, drained
- ½ c. buttered crumbs
- Paprika

Cook yellow squash in salty water until tender. Sauté onion in butter; add flour, salt and milk and cook until thick. Put squash in casserole; layer with cheese and peas. Pour the sauce over next; sprinkle crumbs and paprika on top.

Aunt Pearl, my daddy's sister, brought this to a family reunion many years ago. It is a delicious recipe.

GRANDMA SHAUGHNESSY'S POTATOES

- 5 lb. red potatoes
- 1 c. margarine
- Lawry's seasoning salt

Cube potatoes with skin on. Pace in a 9 x 13 baking dish. Slice margarine in cubes and place over potatoes. Sprinkle heavily with seasoning salt. Bake in 400 degree oven for 1 hour until potatoes are cooked through.

This recipe is from one of my favorite nieces, Stacey Norwood Shaughnessy.

BAKED CHILIES RELLENOS

- 10 whole green chilies, seeded
- ½ lb. Jack cheese, cut in 10 strips
- 1 c. cheddar cheese, grated
- 3 eggs
- ¼ c. flour
- ¾ c. milk
- ¼ t. salt
- ¼ t. pepper
- Dash of Tabasco sauce

Preheat oven to 350 degrees. Cut chilies in half. Spread on paper towel and pat dry. Slip a strip of Jack cheese into each chili and lay them side by side in a greased 9 x 13 baking dish. Sprinkle with cheddar cheese. Beat eggs with flour until smooth. Add milk, seasonings and Tabasco sauce. Pour egg mixture over chilies. Bake uncovered for 45 minutes or until golden brown. Serve with sour cream, salsa and/or guacamole.

BAKED MACARONI + CHEESE

- 8 oz. elbow macaroni
- 4 T. butter
- 4 T. flour
- 2 c. milk
- ½ t. salt
- ¼ t. black pepper
- 2 cups cheddar cheese, shredded
- ½ c. breadcrumbs

Prepare macaroni as directed on package. Melt butter in large sauce pan. Add flour mixed with salt and pepper using a whisk to stir until well blended. Pour milk in gradually stirring constantly. Bring to a boiling point and boil for 2 minutes stirring constantly. Reduce heat and cook 10 minutes stirring constantly. Gradually add shredded cheese and simmer an additional 5 minutes or until cheese melts. Remove from heat and add macaroni to the saucepan; toss to coat with the cheese sauce. Transfer to a buttered baking dish and sprinkle with breadcrumbs. Bake 20 minutes until the top is golden brown in a 400 degree oven.

SHORT CUT LASAGNA

- 1 T. oil
- 1 28 oz. can tomatoes
- 2 envelopes spaghetti mix
- 1 16 oz. pkg. lasagna noodles
- 1 8 oz. pkg. mozzarella cheese, grated
- 1½ lb. ground chuck
- 1 8oz. can tomato sauce
- 2 12 oz. cans V-8 juice
- 1 12 oz. carton cottage cheese
- ¼ c. parmesan cheese
- Chopped parsley

Heat oil in large skillet; add meat and cook, breaking up with a wooden spoon. Stir in tomatoes, V-8 juice, spaghetti sauce mix and tomato sauce. Bring to a boil and simmer 10 minutes. Cover the bottom of an oiled 13x9x2 pan with a small amount of sauce; add a layer of uncooked noodles, cottage cheese and mozzarella cheese. Repeat layers until all ingredients are used, ending with meat sauce. Cover casserole tightly with aluminum foil. Set in a cookie sheet (for spills). Bake one hour at 350 degrees. Remove from oven and let stand 15 minutes. Sprinkle with parmesan cheese and parsley. Cut into squares and serve. Makes approximately 12 servings.

LASAGNA CASSEROLE

Heat in a skillet:

- 2 T. salad oil
- 1 lb. hamburger meat, crumbled.

Add:

- 2 cloves garlic, crushed and browned.
- 1 8oz. can tomato sauce
- 1 16 oz. can tomatoes
- 1½ t. salt
- ¼ t. pepper
- ½ t. oregano.

Cover and simmer for 15 to 20 minutes until it is slightly thickened. Meanwhile, cook 8 oz. of the wide lasagna noodles about 15 minutes in boiling salted water. Drain and rinse. Fill rectangular casserole with alternate layers of noodles, 8 oz. mozzarella cheese slices, 12 oz. ricotta cheese, tomato meat sauce and grated parmesan cheese. Swiss and cottage cheese may be substituted for Italian cheeses. Bake at 375 degrees for 15 to 20 minutes.

CREAM TACOS

Over low heat melt:

- 1 lb. Velveeta cheese
- 1 large can evaporated milk.

At the same time, cook:

- 1½ lb. ground beef
- 1 medium onion, chopped
- 1 large bell pepper, chopped.

Cook until meat is done but not brown. Stir in:

- cheese mixture (from step one)
- 1 can rotel tomatoes, chopped
- 1 8 oz. can tomato sauce
- 1 t. salt
- ½ t. pepper.

Place a layer of tortillas or Doritos in large casserole. Pour in meat mixture. Continue layering until all meat is used ending with meat. Bake at 350 degrees for 30 minutes. (Use large pkg. Doritos or about 18 tortillas. You may use 2 small casseroles and freeze one before baking.)

BEA'S CHICKEN ROTEL

- 3 to 4 pieces of boneless chicken breast
- Water to cover chicken
- 1 t. salt
- 1 small onion, diced
- 1 t. sage
- 1 10 oz. can Rotel tomatoes
- 1 can cream of mushroom soup
- 1 can of the cooked chicken broth
- 1 t. sugar
- 1 c. cheddar cheese, shredded
- Doritos Nacho Cheese chips

In a 13x9 inch baking dish, crumble the chips until they cover the bottom of the dish. Set aside. Boil the chicken with the onion, salt and sage until chicken is tender. In a medium bowl, mix the Rotel, soup, broth and sugar. Stir until blended. Cut chicken into small pieces and spread over the chips. Pour the Rotel mixture over the chicken. Sprinkle cheese on top. Bake in a 350 degree oven for 30 minutes. Note: You may use any kind of chips or cheese, but I found the baked nacho chips to be best.

This recipe is from one of my husband Bill's longtime friends, Juanita Miller McCurdy.

TUNA NOODLE CASSEROLE

- 1 can cream of mushroom soup
- ½ c. milk
- 2 T. chopped pimientos
- 1 c. frozen peas
- 2 5 oz. cans tuna, drained
- 3 oz. medium wide noodles, cooked and drained
- 2 T. plain dry bread crumbs
- 1 T. butter, melted

Heat oven to 400 degrees. Stir soup, milk, pimientos, peas, tuna and noodles in a casserole. Stir the bread crumbs and butter in a small bowl. Bake tune mixture for 20 minutes or until hot and bubbling. Stir tuna mixture and sprinkle with bread crumb mixture. Bake 5 minutes or until bread crumb mixture is golden brown.

BREAKFAST

OVERNIGHT CINNAMON PECAN COFFEE CAKE

This streusel-topped breakfast coffee cake can be prepared and chilled in the pan up to 18 hours before baking.

Streusel Topping:

- ¾ c. brown sugar, firmly packed
- ½ c. pecans, chopped
- 1 t. cinnamon

Coffee Cake:

- ¾ c. butter, softened
- 1 c. sugar
- 2 large eggs
- 2 c. flour
- 1 t. baking powder
- 1 t. soda
- 1 t. nutmeg
- ½ t. salt
- 1 c. sour cream

To prepare streusel topping, combine sugar, pecans and cinnamon in a small bowl.

To prepare cake, beat butter and sugar until light and fluffy; add eggs, one at a time, beating after each addition until combined. In a separate bowl, combine flour, baking powder, soda, nutmeg and salt. Add flour mixture to egg mixture alternately with sour cream and ending with flour mixture. Beat until blended. Spread batter into a greased 13 x 9 pan. Sprinkle streusel topping over batter. Cover with plastic wrap and refrigerate 8 to 18 hours. Bake in a 350 degree oven for 35 minutes or until toothpick inserted in the center comes out clean. Can be served warm or room temperature.

SAUSAGE CASSEROLE

- 6 eggs
- 2 c. milk
- 1 t. salt
- 1 c. cheese, grated
- 4 oz. can sliced mushrooms, drained
- 1 lb. sausage
- 6 slices white bread, cubed
- 1 t. dry mustard

Brown sausage; drain and cool. Beat eggs; add milk, salt and dry mustard and beat again. Stir in bread until mixed. Add sausage, cheese and mushrooms. Put into a greased casserole and refrigerate overnight. Bake in a 350 degree oven for 40 to 45 minutes. Serve with hot biscuits and fruit.

MARGARET'S WAFFLES

- 2 c. flour
- 4 t. baking powder
- ½ t. sugar
- 2 egg **yolks**
- 2 egg whites
- 1¾ c. milk
- ½ c. butter, melted

Sift all dry ingredients together; add milk and beaten egg yolks then melted butter. Fold in stiffly beaten egg whites.

When my children were still at home, we had waffles every Sunday morning. I always worked outside the home, and there wasn't time for waffles during the week. The recipe is from my sister, Margaret Casey.

PANCAKES

- 4 c. flour
- 1 pkg. dry yeast
- 1 t. soda
- ¼ c. canola oil
- 1 qt. buttermilk
- 4 T. baking powder
- 4 eggs

Will keep in the refrigerator for several days.

BUTTERMILK PANCAKES

- 1¼ c. flour
- 1 t. salt
- 1 c. buttermilk
- 5/8 t. soda
- 1 egg

Mix and sift dry ingredients. Beat egg slightly and add to milk. Pour slowly into first mixture. Cook on hot greased griddle.

CHRISTMAS-TREE COFFEE CAKES

- 4 to 4½ c. flour, divided
- ½ c. sugar
- 1½ t. salt
- 2 pkgs. Dry yeast
- ¾ c. milk
- ½ c. water
- ½ c. butter
- 1 egg, slightly beaten
- Filling (recipe follows)
- Glaze (recipe follows)
- Red and green sugar crystals
- Red and green candied cherries (opt.)

Combine 2 c. flour, sugar, salt and yeast in a large mixing bowl; set aside. Combine milk, water and butter in a small saucepan; heat to very warm. Add milk mixture to flour mixture; beat at medium speed of an electric mixer 2 minutes. Add egg and 1 c. remaining flour; beat at high speed 2 minutes, scraping bowl occasionally. Stir in enough flour to make a stiff batter. Cover bowl and chill 8 hours.

Divide dough into 3 equal portions. Turn each portion out onto a lightly floured service and roll each into an 11x10 inch rectangle. Spread one-third of filling over each rectangle, leaving a ½ inch margin around edges. Carefully roll up, jelly roll fashion, beginning at long side. Cut each into 11 (1 inch) slices using an electric knife. Arrange 10 slices on a greased baking sheet in a triangular shape. Center remaining slice at the base of triangle to complete Christmas-tree shape. Repeat procedure with remaining dough to make 2 other cakes. Cover lightly with wax paper sprayed with vegetable cooking spray and let rise in a warm place free from drafts for 1 hour or until doubled in bulk. Bake at 375 degrees for 20 to 25 minutes. Drizzle glaze over rolls while warm. Sprinkle with sugar crystals. Garnish with candied cherries, if desired.

Filling:

- 2 8 oz. cans crushed pineapple, drained
- 2 8 oz. pkgs. cream cheese, softened
- ½ c. sugar
- ¼ t. nutmeg
- 1/8 t. salt

Place pineapple between paper towels to drain excess liquid. Combine cream cheese and remaining ingredients in a mixing bowl; beat at medium speed until blended. Stir in pineapple.

Glaze:

- 2 c. powdered sugar, sifted
- 3 T. milk

Combine sugar and milk in a small bowl; beat at medium speed until blended.

QUICHE LORRAINE WITH HAM

- Unbaked 9" pastry shell
- 4 slices bacon, cooked and crumbled
- ¼ medium onion, diced and sautéed until soft
- 8 slices ham, shredded
- 8 paper thin slices Swiss cheese
- 3 eggs
- ¼ t. dry mustard
- 1 c. heavy cream, heated
- Nutmeg

Heat oven to 350 degrees. Sprinkle bacon and onion over bottom of pie crust. Add half of ham; put 4 slices of cheese over ham. Add rest of ham and cheese on top. Beat eggs and mustard; add hot cream and continue beating. Pour over ham and cheese. Let stand 10 minutes. Sprinkle a tiny bit of nutmeg on top and bake 30 to 35 minutes until custard is set.

This recipe is from Wanda Johns, a very dear friend.

BEEF

SWISS STEAK

Cut round steak into serving size pieces and season with salt and pepper. Place steak in a deep skillet. Slice onions and green peppers on top of it and pour 1 can of tomatoes over it. Cover and bake at 350 degrees for 1¼ hours.

MANICOTTI

- 1 lb. ground chuck beef
- 1 c. small curd cottage cheese
- 4 oz. mozzarella cheese, grated
- 2 eggs
- 3 T. canned milk
- ¾ t. salt
- ¼ t. pepper
- 1/8 t. garlic powder
- 1 pkg. manicotti shells

Mix ingredients thoroughly and let set. Cook manicotti shells per package directions.

Sauce:

Use one package American Beauty Italian Style spaghetti sauce mix and 1 15 oz. can tomato sauce and ½ can water. Cook as directed on package.

Stuff shells with meat mixture and place in buttered baking dish. Cover with sauce and bake for 35 to 45 minutes in a 350 degree oven.

HAMBURGER STROGANOFF

- ½ c. onion, finely copped
- ¼ c. butter
- 1 lb. ground beef
- 1 c. sour cream
- 1 c. sliced mushrooms
- 2 T. flour
- 2 t. salt
- 1 t. pepper
- ¼ t. paprika
- 1 c. cream of chicken soup

Cook the onion in butter in a saucepan over medium heat until transparent. Add the beef and cook stirring until meat is light brown. Add the flour, salt, pepper, mushrooms and soup and cook for 5 minutes. Add the sour cream and simmer for 15 minutes longer. Serve over rice or egg noodles and garnish with paprika. Do not let cream boil.

FAVORITE MEAT LOAF

- 2 lbs. ground beef
- ½ c. onion, chopped
- 2/3 c. bread crumbs
- 1 egg, beaten
- ½ 8 oz. can tomato sauce
- 2 t. salt
- ¼ t. pepper
- ½ t. dry mustard
- 2 t. Worcestershire sauce

Mix these ingredients thoroughly. Put into loaf pan or casserole. Now combine the remaining tomato sauce, ½ c. water, 2 T. brown sugar, 2 T. vinegar, 1 t. Worcestershire sauce and 2 t. dry mustard. Pour this spicy mixture over top of meatloaf and bake at 325 degrees for at least 1 ½ hours.

Sometime during the 1960's, this recipe was given to me from my sister, Eunice (now deceased) who lived in California.

TOSSED TACOS

Sauce:

- 1 lb. ground meat
- 1 medium onion, chopped
- 1 can tomatoes and green chilies

Simmer for 10 to 15 minutes.

Mix in bowl:

- ½ head lettuce, chopped
- 2 tomatoes, diced
- 8 oz. cheese, grated
- 1 regular size bag Fritos, crushed

Pour sauce over salad mixture and toss until mixed.

BRISKET

Mix: 1 pkg. dry onion soup, 2 c. hot water, 1/3 c. lemon juice, ¼ c. soy sauce and 3T. liquid smoke. Pour the mixture over brisket and bake at 300 degrees in foil covered pan for about one hour per pound or until tender. Note: If you have a crock pot, cook on high temperature for 45 minutes to an hour, then slow cook. The soup mix will be enough for 2 to 14 lbs. of meat.

SMOKED BRISKET

- 5 to 6 lb. boneless beef brisket
- 1/3 c. liquid smoke
- Worcestershire sauce
- Seasoned salt
- Garlic salt
- Salt and pepper
- ¾ c. BBQ sauce

Place meat in baking dish and pour liquid smoke and a little Worcestershire sauce over brisket. Sprinkle meat generously on both sides with seasoned salt and garlic salt. Cover with foil and place in refrigerator overnight. When ready to bake, sprinkle both sides with salt and pepper. Replace foil and bake for 5 hours at 275 degrees. Pour ¾ c. of BBQ sauce over meat and bake for 1 hour longer.

TERIAKI STEAK

Cut a round steak in strips and marinate in a mixture of 2/3 c. sugar, 1 c. soy sauce, 1 clove garlic and 1 t. ginger. Marinate all day turning often. Put on skewers and grill.

LAYERED MEXICAN MEAL

- Doritos
- Chili
- Refried Beans
- Cheddar cheese, grated
- Monterrey Jack cheese, grated
- Onions, chopped
- Tomatoes, chopped
- Lettuce, chopped
- Black olives, sliced
- Sour Cream
- Avocado Dip

Layer on your plate in order as listed. (Back in the olden days before it was politically incorrect, we called this Wetback. We first started fixing this in the early 1950's.) We use homemade chili for this recipe.

COMPANY CASSEROLE

- 1½ lbs. ground chuck
- 1 8 oz. pkg. egg noodles
- 1 16 oz. can tomato sauce
- 1 c. cottage cheese
- 1 c. sour cream
- 1 c. cheddar cheese, divided
- 6 green onions, chopped
- ½ small green pepper, chopped
- 2 T. garlic powder
- 2 t. salt
- 1½ t. ground black pepper
- 1 T. butter

Preheat oven to 350 degrees. Cook the noodles according to package instructions, drain and set aside. Melt butter in a medium-sized skillet set at medium high and sauté green pepper. Add meat and cook until brown. Drain if necessary. In a mixing bowl, combine meat-pepper mixture and add salt, pepper, garlic powder, tomato sauce, green onions, cottage cheese, one half of cheddar cheese, sour cream and noodles. Transfer mixture to a two-quart casserole. Top with remaining cheese and bake until cheese is melted, 15 to 20 minutes.

ITALIAN MEATLOAF

- 1½ slices of white bread
- 3 T. milk
- ½ medium yellow onion, chopped
- 8 ounces button mushrooms, chopped
- 1½ lbs. ground chuck
- 1 egg
- ½ c. grated Parmigiano Reggiano cheese
- 1 t. salt
- Freshly ground black pepper
- 12 cherry tomatoes, cut into halves

Preheat oven to 375 degrees. Combine milk and bread. Soak 5 minutes. Combine bread mixture, onion, mushrooms, beef, egg, cheese, salt, pepper and half the tomatoes. Mix with your hands. Shape into a loaf and place in a baking dish. Scatter with remaining tomatoes. Bake 40 minutes or until meat register 160 degrees.

CHICKEN

STIR FRY CHICKEN

- 2 T. peanut oil
- boneless-skinless chicken breasts cut into chunks or strips

Cook in wok for a few minutes. Chicken can be marinated in soy sauce prior to cooking.

Add vegetables:

- Onion
- red pepper
- green pepper
- zucchini
- broccoli
- can of Chinese vegetables (rinse and drain)
- can of baby corn (rinse and drain).

Serve with soy sauce over rice.

You can vary vegetables –water chestnuts, snow peas etc.

ALOHA CHICKEN

- ½ c. soy sauce
- 2 T. honey
- ½ bunch green onions, chopped

Marinate chicken pieces overnight in sauce. Bake in sauce for 1 hour at 350 degrees.

POTATO CHIP CHICKEN

Melt together in a sauce pan:

- 1 cube of margarine or butter
- Salt
- Pepper
- garlic salt.

Mash 1 large bag of chips until crumbly. Put chicken in butter and roll in crumbs. Place in a flat pan and bake at 325 degrees for about one hour.

TERIAKI CHICKEN

- 8 chicken breasts, boneless and skinless
- ¾ c. soy sauce
- ½ c. water
- ½ t. garlic powder
- ¼ t. ginger
- ½ t. rosemary
- 6 to 8 t. sweetener

Pour over chicken. Marinate for 2 hours. Bake or charcoal.

ORIENTAL CHICKEN

- 8 chicken breasts, boneless and skinless
- 1 bottle thousand island salad dressing
- 1 10 oz. jar apricot jam
- 1 pkg. dry onion soup mix

Mix dressing, jam and soup mix and pour mixture over top of chicken which has been placed in a buttered casserole. Bake in a 400 degree oven for one hour. This can be cooked in crock pot on low for 6 hours. Serve over rice.

CURRIED CHICKEN

- Chicken breasts
- ¼ c. margarine
- 1 can chicken broth
- 3 T. margarine
- ¼ t. pepper
- 1 clove garlic
- 2 t. grated lime
- ¼ t. cardamom
- 1 t. salt
- 2 t. curry powder
- 2 t. lemon juice
- 1 c. chopped apple
- ¼ c. flour

- 1 t. ginger

Brown chicken breasts (I use boneless skinless) 5 minutes on each side in ¼ c. margarine. Add 1 can chicken broth and bring to a boil. Reduce heat and add remaining ingredients. Simmer covered 20 minutes. Serve over yellow rice.

ELLEN'S CHICKEN BREASTS AND WILD RICE

- Boned chicken breasts, remove skin and then salt chicken breasts

Mix:

- 1 egg
- ¼ c. milk

Dip chicken in mixture and roll in flour

Fry in Crisco oil until golden brown, remove from oil and drain on paper towels. Mix can of cream of mushroom soup with ½ can milk. Place chicken in casserole dish and cover with soup mixture. Bake until done at 350 degrees, approximately 45 to 50 minutes. Prepare wild and long grain rice according to package directions. Serve chicken over rice. Serve hot.

OVEN-FRIED CHICKEN CUTLETS

- 1/3 c. butter or margarine, melted
- 1 T. Dijon mustard
- ¼ t. garlic powder
- ¼ t. salt
- ¼ t. pepper
- 1 c. round buttery cracker crumbs, about 44 crackers
- ½ c. grated Parmesan cheese
- 4 chicken breast cutlets, about 1¼ lbs.
- Garnish: fresh parsley, chopped

Stir together first 5 ingredients in a medium bowl. Combine cracker crumbs and cheese in a shallow bowl. Dip chicken in butter mixture; dredge in cracker crumb mixture. Place on a foil-lined baking sheet. Bake at 400 degrees for 25 to 30 minutes or until chicken is brown and done. Garnish, if desired.

CHICKEN SPAGHETTI

Cook frying chicken in 1 qt. water until very tender (simmer about 1 hr.) then add:

- a few celery tops
- ½ t. salt
- ¼ t. pepper
- bay leaf.

Simmer 30 minutes more and let cool in pan.

Chicken

Sauté in 1 stick of butter:

- 1 finely minced onion
- 3 finely minced inner celery stalks
- ½ shredded green pepper

Then add:

- 1 pt. chicken broth from chicken
- 1 28 oz. can diced tomatoes drained
- ½ t. salt
- ¼ t. pepper
- 2 T. fresh parsley or 2 t. dried parsley
- 1 T. Worcestershire sauce
- dash of cayenne pepper.

Cook until thick about 30 minutes then add 1 small can mushrooms and 1 small can sliced black olives. Meanwhile, boil 10 oz. spaghetti in boiling water with 1½ t. oil and ½ t. salt for 6 to 8 minutes. Place in casserole, spaghetti, chicken and sauce in layers until all used. Dust lightly with cracker crumbs. Dot with water. Bake 350 degrees for 45 minutes. (Should be moist so use more broth if necessary.)

This recipe is from one of my dearest longtime friends, Virgie Cartner.

LEFTOVER CHICKEN OR TURKEY POT PIE

- 4 T. butter
- 1 small onion, chopped
- 2 medium carrots, peeled and thinly sliced
- 1 rib celery, thinly sliced
- Kosher salt and pepper
- 4 T. flour
- 2½ c. chicken or turkey broth, warmed
- ¼ c. heavy cream
- ¾ t. dried thyme
- 1½ c. meat, cooked and shredded chicken or turkey
- ½ c. frozen peas
- 2 T. chopped parsley
- 1 sheet frozen puff pastry, thawed
- 1 large egg

Preheat oven to 375 degrees. Warm butter in a large saucepan over medium heat. Add onion, carrot and celery, sprinkle with salt and pepper, and cook, stirring occasionally, until tender but not browned, 10 minutes. Sprinkle flour over vegetables and cook 3 minutes, stirring frequently. Whisk in broth and cream. Add thyme. Bring to a simmer, then reduce heat to medium-low and simmer about 8 minutes, until mixture is thickened. Season with salt and pepper. Remove from heat and stir in meat, peas and parsley. This may be cooked in ramekins or a casserole placed on a baking sheet. Place pastry (I prefer pie crust rather than puff pastry) over dish. In a small bowl, whisk egg with 1 T. water. Brush pastry with egg mixture. Bake until pastry is deep gold and the filling bubbles about 35 minutes. Let stand 5 minutes before serving.

OVEN-FRIED CHICKEN

- 4 chicken breast, boneless skinless
- 1 c. panko bread crumbs
- ¾ t. paprika
- ½ rounded t. dried thyme
- 1½ c. buttermilk
- 2 t. salt, divided
- ½ c. onion, coarsely grated
- 1 t. black pepper, divided
- 2 ¼ t. dried mustard
- 2 T. white vinegar

Mix buttermilk, ½ t. salt, onion, ¾ t. pepper, dried mustard and vinegar. Add chicken, cover and refrigerate overnight. Preheat oven to 425 degrees. Combine panko bread crumbs, paprika, remaining salt and pepper and thyme. Remove chicken from marinade and dredge pieces in panko mixture. Spray all sides with cooking spray. Place in pan and bake 35 to 45 minutes or until done.

MEXICAN CHICKEN

- 4 cooked chicken breasts, boneless skinless
- 10 corn tortillas, torn in pieces
- 1 7 oz. can diced green chilies
- 1 7 oz. can green chili salsa
- 1 can cream of mushroom soup
- 1 can cream of chicken soup
- 1½ c. cheese, grated (use jack or cheddar)

Mix chilies, salsa and soups and layer with diced chicken. Repeat layer. Put cheese on top and cover and chill for 8 hours or overnight. Cook uncovered at 350 degrees for 30 minutes.

PORK

ROASTED MARINATED PORK TENDERLOIN

- 2 (1 lb. each) pork tenderloins
- ½ c. cooking sherry
- ½ c. soy sauce
- 2 large cloves garlic, minced
- 1 T. dry mustard
- 1 t. ground ginger
- 1 t. crushed thyme

In a bowl, combine all ingredients except the pork to create the marinade. Put raw pork tenderloins and marinate mixture in a large plastic food storage bag, refrigerate at least 2 hours or overnight.

Preheat oven to 325 degrees. Spray a baking dish with non-stick cooking spray and place pork and marinade into the dish. Bake uncovered (basting periodically) for 40 to 45 minutes or until your meat thermometer reaches 160 degrees. Remove pork from baking dish and let stand for 10 minutes before slicing. Keep the marinade mixture warm over low heat. This roasted marinated pork goes great with steamed broccoli and wild rice.

COUNTRY STYLE RIBS

Put ribs in crock pot with 2 cups beef bouillon. Cook on high all day. Serve with:

SAUERKRAUT WITH APPLES

- 1 27 oz. can sauerkraut
- 2 T. bacon drippings
- 1 large potato, shredded
- 2 T. brown sugar
- 1 t. caraway seed
- 1 medium onion, sliced
- 3 medium apples, peeled and sliced
- 1 c. chicken broth
- 1 t. salt

Drain and snip sauerkraut. Cook onion in bacon drippings until tender. Add sauerkraut, apples, potato, broth, brown sugar, salt and caraway seed. Mix well. Cover and cook 15 to 20 minutes. Add more broth if needed. Sprinkle with additional brown sugar if desired.

CROCK POT PULLED PORK

- 1 18 oz. bottle barbecue sauce
- 1 large onion, finely chopped
- 1 3 lb. boneless pork roast

Put all ingredients in slow cooker and cook on low for 8 to 10 hours. Remove meat from cooker. Using 2 forks, pull or shred the pork. Return to cooker and cook on low for and additional hour or two for more flavor.

SHANE'S BABY BACK RIBS

- 4 lbs. baby back ribs
- 5 T. sugar
- 3 T. honey
- 3 T. soy sauce
- 2 T. catsup
- 1 t. salt
- 1 c. hot chicken broth

Mix ingredients and soak the ribs for 2 hours. Bake in oven at 300 degrees for 2 to 3 hours. Baste often with the sauce. If ribs are fatty, drop them in boiling water for about 5 minutes before marinating then proceed as directed.

This was Shane's (my first grandchild) favorite when he was growing up. He is now a Chef in Denver, Colorado.

His recipes are fancier than mine, but he will still receive a cookbook.

HAM AND POTATO CASSEROLE

- 6 T. butter, melted
- 6 T. flour
- ¾ t. salt.
- 3 c. milk
- 3 c. sharp cheddar cheese, shredded
- 4 unpeeled potatoes, sliced very thin
- ½ c. onion, chopped
- 4 c. ham, cubed

Stir flour and salt into melted butter and gradually add the milk. Heat on medium for 6 minutes in microwave. Stir well and heat again for 2 minutes until thicker. Stir in the cheese and heat until smooth. Set aside. In a large casserole, place 1/2 of the potatoes, sprinkle salt and pepper over potatoes, and add ½ the onion, ham and cheese sauce. Repeat layer. Cover with foil and bake at 375 degrees for 30 minutes. Uncover and bake 30 to 45 more minutes.

HAWAIIN PORK CHOPS

- 6 pork chops, ¾ inch thick
- 1½ c. instant rice
- 1 small can crushed pineapple
- 1 c. orange juice
- 1 can chicken with rice soup
- 1/3 c. brown sugar

Brown chops and season with salt and pepper. Spread rice in bottom of baking pan. Place chops on rice. Pour the can of soup, orange juice and pineapple over chops. Sprinkle brown sugar on top. Cover and bake at 350 degrees for 45 minutes. Uncover and bake for 10 more minutes. This is Bill's creation!

SEAFOOD & FISH

SHRIMP CREOLE

- 1 c. onions, sliced
- ½ c. celery, diced
- ½ t. garlic, minced
- 3 T. oil
- 1 T. flour
- 1 t. salt
- 1 t. sugar
- 1 T. chili powder
- 1 c. water
- 2 c. canned tomatoes
- 2 c. peas
- 1 T. vinegar
- 2 c. cooked shrimp
- 4 c. rice

Cook onion, celery and garlic in oil until tender. Add flour, salt, sugar and chili powder which have been mixed with ¼ c. water. Add remaining water and simmer uncovered over low heat for 15 minutes. Add tomatoes, peas, vinegar and shrimp. Heat. Serve over rice.

This recipe is from my favorite daughter-in-law, Tracy Holmes.

CRAB SUPREME

- 8 slices white bread
- 2 c. crab meat
- 1 onion, chopped
- ½ c. green pepper, chopped
- 1 c. celery, chopped
- ½ c. mayonnaise
- 4 eggs, beaten
- 3 c. milk
- 1 can cream of mushroom soup
- 1/3 c. sherry
- Cheese, grated
- Paprika

Cook celery slowly in a small amount of water. Drain. Dice half the bread into baking dish. (Cut off crusts and do not use) Mix the crab, onion, green pepper, celery and mayonnaise and spread over bread. Dice other slices of bread and place over crab mixture. Mix eggs, milk and sherry and pour over dish. Cover and place in refrigerator overnight. Bake for 15 minutes at 325 degrees. Then spoon soup over top and sprinkle with cheese and paprika. Bake one hour or until golden brown. Note: You can use canned crab. (Use snow crab).

PASTA WITH LEMON AND SHRIMP

- 1 9 oz. pkg. Buitoni Refrigerated linguine
- 8 oz. medium shrimp
- 1 7 oz. Buitoni Refrigerated pesto with basil
- 1½ t. grated lemon peel
- 2 T. green onion, finely sliced

Prepare linguine according to package directions, drain and keep warm. Cook shrimp and keep warm. Combine pesto and lemon peel in medium saucepan and cook over medium-low heat for 6 to 8 minutes stirring frequently. Transfer cooked pasta to serving plates. Top with sauce and shrimp. Sprinkle with green onions.

SALMON PATTIES

- 1 7 oz. can salmon
- 8 soda crackers, crumbled
- 1 egg
- 1 T. onion, grated
- 1 T. parsley
- 1 t. dry mustard
- Salt
- Celery, chopped
- 1 T. lemon juice

Drain salmon, reserving liquid. Flake and clean salmon and blend it with the reserved liquid and the remaining ingredients. Add more crackers or another egg if the consistency will not make firm patties. After you make the patties, fry them in a skillet. Fry with 2 to 3 tablespoon melted butter. Brown on both sides. Serve with sliced lemon wedges.

OVEN FRIED FISH

- 2 lbs. fish fillets
- 1 T. fresh lemon juice
- ¼ c. skim milk
- 1 t. fresh garlic, minced
- ¼ t. black pepper
- ¼ t. salt
- ¼ t. onion powder
- ½ c. panko crumbs
- 1 T. cooking oil
- Hot pepper sauce to taste

Heat oven to 475 degrees. Wipe fillets with lemon juice and pat dry with paper towel. In bowl, combine milk, pepper sauce and garlic. On plate, combine pepper, salt, onion powder and crumbs. Dip fillets in milk and coat with crumb mixture, pressing crumbs into the fillet. Spread 1 T. oil in shallow baking dish. Arrange fish in the dish. Bake for about 20 minutes on middle rack of oven. Fish will be brown and crisp on the outside, but flakey and moist on the inside.

SALMON AND CORN PIE

- 3 T. butter
- 3 T. flour
- ½ t. salt
- Dash of pepper
- 2 c. milk
- 1 can salmon
- 2 T. onion, minced
- 1 c. cheese, grated
- 1 can corn, drained
- ½ c. buttered crumbs

Make a white sauce with butter, flour, seasonings and milk. Pick over and flake salmon. Place 1/3 of the salmon in a buttered casserole, add 1/3 of the white sauce to which the onion has been added and sprinkle with 1/3 of the grated cheese. Repeat the layers twice. Spread the corn over top and sprinkle with buttered crumbs. Bake at 350 degrees for about 20 minutes.

DESSERTS

CHOCOLATE DELIGHT

Crust:

- 1 c. flour
- 1 stick melted butter or margarine
- 1 c. finely chopped pecans.

Mix and then spread into 9x13 baking pan. Bake at 350 degrees for 20 minutes. Cool.

Filling:

- 1 c. frozen whipped topping
- 1 c. powdered sugar
- 1 8 oz. pkg. cream cheese
- 1 3 oz. pkg. instant vanilla pudding
- 1 3 oz. pkg. instant chocolate pudding
- 3 c. milk
- 3. c. frozen whipped topping
- 1 milk chocolate candy bar

Mix 1 c. whipped topping and 1 c. powdered sugar and the cream cheese. Spread over the cooled crust. Mix 1½ c. milk to each pudding mix and let set to thicken. Pour chocolate pudding over cream cheese. Pour vanilla over chocolate pudding. Top with the 3 c. whipped topping. Sprinkle with grated frozen chocolate candy bar. (I prefer whipping cream instead of frozen whipped topping.)

BANANA PUDDING

- 14 oz. can sweetened condensed milk
- 1½ c. ice water
- 3½ oz. pkg. instant vanilla pudding mix
- 1 8 oz. carton cool whip (I use whipped cream)

Combine milk and ice water. Add pudding mix and beat. Chill 5 minutes. Fold in cool whip. Layer with vanilla wafers, sliced bananas, sliced strawberries (opt.) and pudding mixture. Top with cool whip.

ANGEL JELL-O

- 2 pkgs. strawberry Jell-O
- 2½ c. hot water
- 2 t. sugar

Mix and let cool. Add 1 box frozen strawberries. Set aside.

Beat 1 c. whipping cream and fold into Jell-O.

Break an angel food cake into small bits and place in bottom of oblong pan. Pour gelatin mixture over it. Refrigerate overnight and cut into squares.

Apple Dumplings (1)

Pastry:

- 2¼ c. flour
- ¾ t. salt
- ¾ c. shortening
- 6 to 8 T. ice water

Mix and roll pastry. Cut in squares. Set aside.

Syrup:

- 1 c. sugar
- 1 t. cinnamon
- 4 T. butter
- 2 C. water

Boil 3 minutes. Set aside.

Filling Mix:

- 6 apples, peeled and sliced
- ½ c. sugar
- 1½ t. cinnamon
- 1 T. butter

Place apples in square of dough. Bring corners up and seal. Place 2 inches apart in baking pan. Pour hot syrup around dumplings. Bake 5 to 7 minutes at 500 degrees until crust is slightly browned. Reduce heat to 350 degrees. Bake 30 to 35 minutes longer.

This is one my mother's recipes.

APPLE DUMPLINGS (2)

- 2 eight roll cans crescent rolls
- 2 Granny Smith apples
- ¾ c. butter or margarine
- 1½ c. sugar
- 2 t. cinnamon
- 2 t. vanilla
- 12 oz. can mountain dew

Peel and slice apples into 8 slices each. Wrap and seal each slice in a crescent roll. Place in greased 12x9 pan. Melt butter and mix in the sugar, cinnamon and vanilla. Pour over the rolls. Pour mountain dew over all. Bake 350 degrees for about 40 minutes.

Robbie Rains fixed this recipe and brought it to a Ladies Bible class luncheon. It was so good! She shared it with me.

ICE CREAM-TOFFEE DESSERT

- 2 3 oz. pkgs. ladyfingers
- 2 T. instant coffee granules
- ¼ c. hot water
- 6 1.4 oz. toffee candy bars, divided
- ½ gal. Vanilla ice cream, softened
- 3 T. coffee liqueur (opt.)
- 1 8 oz. container frozen whipped topping, thawed

Stand lady fingers around edge of 9 inch spring form pan; line bottom of pan with remaining ladyfingers. Combine coffee and ¼ c. hot water in a small bowl, stirring until dissolved; let cool completely. Chop 5 candy bars into small pieces. Stir chopped candy and coffee into ice cream. Spoon into prepared pan. Cover with plastic wrap and freeze 8 hours. Stir liqueur into whipped topping, if desired. Dollop around edge of ice-cream mixture. Chop remaining candy bar and sprinkle evenly over top. Let stand 30 minutes before serving.

CHERRIES IN THE SNOW

- 8 oz. cream cheese (room temperature)
- 1 c. powdered sugar
- 1 18 oz. carton whipped topping (I use whipping cream)
- Angel food cake
- 2 can cherry pie filling

Beat cream cheese and powdered sugar until smooth. Fold mixture into whipped topping. Put half of mixture into bottom of 9x12 pan. Add a layer of angel food cake cut into ½ inch strips. Top with remaining mixture and spread pie filling on top. Refrigerate.

APRICOT DESSERT

Butter a baking dish and sprinkle a layer of vanilla wafer crumbs in bottom of dish.

Add in Order:

1st layer: Boil for 1 minute:

- 4 stiffly beaten eggs
- 2 cubes soft margarine
- 2 c. powdered sugar.

Stir constantly while cooking to keep from burning.

2nd layer: 2 can apricot halves, face up

3rd layer: 1 c. whipping cream, sweetened and beaten until peaks form.

4th layer: Sprinkle 1 c. broken pecans over whipped cream.

5th layer: Cover with layer of vanilla wafer crumbs.

Refrigerate 24 hours. Cut in squares.

DATE PUDDING

- 1 c. chopped dates
- 1 c. chopped nuts
- 1 c. sugar
- 2 eggs, separated
- 2 T. flour
- 1 t. baking powder
- 2 T. milk

Mix dates, nuts and sugar. Add flour sifted with baking powder. Add milk and beaten egg yolks. Last fold in stiffly beaten egg whites. Place in buttered pan and bake at 300 degrees for 20 to 30 minutes.

After I retired, I was a nanny to a precious little girl, Kendall Phillips. I took care of her from the time she was born until she was 5 years of age. Her mother, Dr. Diane Heaton Phillips, gave me this recipe which had been given to her from her grandmother. I took care of Kendall until one week before I married Bill and moved to Shawnee, Oklahoma. I had 5 happy years with Kendall, and Bill and I will celebrate 6 happy years July 4, 2015. (Lord willing.)

QUICK PUMPKIN MUFFINS

- 1 15 oz. pkg. yellow cake mix
- 1 15 oz. can pumpkin
- 1 7 oz. pkg. Milky Way Simply Caramel Bites
- 4 oz. cream cheese, softened
- 1/3 c. powdered sugar
- 1 T. milk

Preheat oven to 350 degrees. Combine cake mix and pumpkin in a mixing bowl. Using an electric mixer, beat on high speed 2 minutes, scraping sides of bowl after 1 minute. Batter will be thick. Line a muffin tin with 12 deep paper liners. Spoon batter into cups ¾ full. Push 3 candies into the center of each cup and swirl batter around top to cover candy and make a smooth top. Bake 17 to 20 minutes, until a toothpick inserted in the center comes out clean. Let cool slightly before serving. (The caramels will be hot.) To make icing, whisk cream cheese, powdered sugar and milk together until smooth. Drizzle on top of cooled muffins. Makes 1 dozen.

HERRY TORTE DESSERT

- 1 can cherries
- 1 small can crushed pineapple
- 1½ c. sugar
- 1/3 c. cornstarch

Cook juice, sugar and cornstarch until clear; add cherries, pineapple and red food coloring. Cook until thick. Prepare a crust with 1 c. quick cooking oatmeal, 2 c. flour, 1 c. Wheaties or bran flakes, 1 c. brown sugar, 1 t. soda, ¼ t. salt, ¾ c. melted butter and 1½ t. vanilla. Put ½ crust mixture in pan and pat down. Put in cherry mixture (mixture should still be warm or it will stick). Sprinkle other half of crust mixture over the top. Bake at 375 degrees for 20 to 25 minutes. Serve with ice cream or whipped cream.

CAKES

LAUREN'S BIRTHDAY CAKE

- 1 pkg. strawberry Jell-O
- ½ c. water
- ½ c. Wesson oil
- 1 pkg. white cake mix
- 4 eggs
- ½ c. frozen strawberries

Beat all ingredients together except eggs and strawberries for 4 minutes at medium speed. Add eggs one at a time and beat well. Add strawberries and beat again. Pour into 3 8 inch greased and floured pans. Bake at 325 degrees for 30 to 40 minutes.

Frosting:

- ¼ lb. soft butter
- 1 box powdered sugar
- ½ c. strawberries.

This has always been my Granddaughter Lauren's favorite birthday cake, and she is one of my favorites, too.

FRESH APPLE CAKE

Mix:

- 1½ c. oil
- 2 c. sugar

Add:

- 3 eggs

Sift together and add:

- 3 c. flour
- 1 t. salt
- 1½ t. soda
- ½ t. cinnamon
- ½ t. cloves
- ½ t. Nutmeg

Add:

- 1 t. vanilla
- 3 c. apples, chopped
- 2 c. nuts, chopped

Bake in a grease and floured tube pan for 1½ hours. Bake 1 hour at 350 degrees, then reduce heat to 300 degrees for remaining ½ hour.

LEMON SUPREME CAKE

- 1 box lemon cake mix
- ½ c. sugar
- ¾ c. oil
- 1 c. apricot nectar
- 4 eggs

Mix cake mix, sugar, oil and nectar together. Add eggs one at a time. Bake in tube pan at 325 degrees for one hour. Mix one cup powdered sugar and the juice of 1 lemon. To make a glaze, pour mixture over cake while it is still warm.

LEMON CAKE

Mix:

- 1 pkg. white or yellow cake mix
- 1 pkg. lemon Jell-O

Stir in

- 2/3 c. water
- 2/3 c. salad oil
- 3 eggs.

Beat until smooth. Bake in an oblong pan. When done, remove from oven and stick full of holes. Prepare a sauce of 2½ c. powdered sugar, ¾ cube of butter and 2 to 3 lemons. Spoon over cake immediately.

DREAM CAKE

- 1 cake mix, pineapple, lemon or chocolate
- 1 pkg. instant pudding mix, pineapple, lemon or chocolate
- ½ c. Wesson oil
- 1 c. water
- 4 fresh eggs

Mix all together until blended; beat 2 minutes. Cook in greased tube pan for 45 to 55 minutes at 375 degrees. Let cool in pan, right side up, for 25 minutes. Glaze: 2 T. milk, 1 c. powdered sugar.

DUMP CAKE

Grease a 13x11½ inch pan.

- Spread 1 can crushed pineapple (drained) in pan
- Top with 1 can cherry pie filling.
- Sprinkle 1 pkg. yellow cake mix on top.
- Add 1 c. chopped nuts.
- Lay 1½ sticks of margarine (sliced in pats) across top.

Bake in a 350 degree oven for a little over an hour or until toothpick inserted in middle comes out clean. Serve warm with whipped cream.

COCONUT CREAM CAKE

- 2 c. flaked coconut
- 2 c. sour cream
- 1½ c. sugar
- 1 pkg. white cake mix
- 1 8 oz. carton cool whip

Mix coconut, sour cream and sugar; chill overnight. Prepare and bake cake mix according to package directions; cool layers and split each layer in half horizontally. Reserve 1 c. of sour cream mixture. Spread remaining sour cream mixture between cake layers. Mix the 1 c. reserved mixture with whipped topping. Use to frost top and sides of cake. Seal in air tight container and chill overnight.

PUMPKIN CRUNCH CAKE

- 1 16 oz. can pumpkin
- 1 12 oz. can evaporated milk
- 1½ c. sugar
- 2 t. pumpkin pie spice
- 1 t. salt
- 4 eggs
- 1 box yellow cake mix
- 1 c. pecans, chopped
- 1 c. butter

Preheat oven to 350 degrees. Grease 9x13 inch baking dish. In a large bowl, beat pumpkin, milk, sugar, spice, salt and eggs until well mixed. Spread in prepared baking dish. Sprinkle dry cake mix over mixture. Sprinkle pecans evenly over cake mix. Thinly slice butter and place on top of pecans. Do not stir. Bake 50 minutes until golden brown on top. Serve warm with whipped cream.

MANDARIN ORANGE CAKE

- 1 butter cake mix
- ½ c. oil
- 4 eggs
- 1 small can mandarin oranges with juice, smashed with a fork

Beat together. Bake in 3 layers at 350 degrees for 15 to 20 minutes.

Frosting:

- 1 lg. can crushed pineapple with juice
- 1 sm. pkg. instant vanilla pudding
- 1 sm. container cool whip

Fold together and frost.

Note: Better a few days old.

BLUEBERRY CRUNCH

- 1 21 oz. can blueberry pie filling
- 1 15 oz. can crushed pineapple
- 1 pkg. yellow cake mix
- 1 c. nuts, chopped
- 1 c. butter, melted

Preheat oven to 350 degrees. In a 9x13 inch pan, layer blueberry pie filling and pineapple; stir lightly. Sprinkle evenly with dry cake mix. Cover with chopped nuts. Drizzle top with melted butter. Bake 35 to 40 minutes or until golden brown.

CHEESE CAKE

Mix 1 pkg. lemon Jell-O and 1 c. boiling water; chill until set.

Cream 1 8 oz. pkg. cream cheese, ½ c. sugar and 1 t. vanilla, and add the Jell-O and blend.

Whip 1 tall can Minot and fold into mixture. Pour into graham cracker crust made with 3 c. graham cracker crumbs and ½ c. melted margarine.

APPLE CAKE

- 2 eggs
- 1/2 cup margarine
- 2½ c. flour
- 1½ t. soda
- 2 c. sugar
- 3 c. tart apples, cut into small pieces
- 3 t. cinnamon
- 1 c. buttermilk

Cream sugar and margarine, add eggs one at a time, beating well. Sift dry ingredients, add flour and milk alternately to first mixture. Add apples last. Pour mixture into a 9x13 lightly greased pan. Bake at 350 degrees for 45 minutes.

Topping:

- 1 c. coconut
- ½ c. evaporated milk
- ½ t. vanilla
- 2/3 c. brown sugar
- 6 T. margarine

Cream sugar and margarine, add milk, vanilla and coconut. Spread over cake and return to oven long enough for sugar to melt. This is better the second day than the first.

This is one of my Mother's recipes.

BARBARA JOINER'S CHEESECAKE

- 3 8 oz. pkgs. cream cheese
- 6 eggs
- 1½ c. sugar
- 2 t. vanilla

Use cream cheese and eggs at room temperature. Cream the cheese with sugar. Add egg yolks, then vanilla. Whip egg whites until very stiff but not dry. Fold whites into mixture. Pour into graham cracker crust. Bake 55 minutes at 325 degrees.

Sour Cream Mixture: ½ c. sour cream, 2 T. powdered sugar and ½ t. vanilla. Pour over top and bake 5 minutes more.

PRUNE CAKE

Cream:

- 1 cup Wesson oil
- 1½ c. sugar
- 1 c. buttermilk

Sift together the following ingredients and then mix with the creamed items:

- 2 c. flour
- 1 t. soda
- 1 t. salt

- ½ t. allspice
- ½ t. nutmeg
- 1 t. cinnamon

Add:

- 3 unbeaten eggs
- 1 t. vanilla
- 1 c. nuts

Fold in 1 c. stewed prunes

Bake 45 minutes at 350 degrees.

Icing: About 5 minutes before cake is done, cook together:

- 1 c. sugar
- 2 T. butter
- ½ c. buttermilk

Boil 5 minutes. Remove from heat and add ½ t. soda then pour over cake as soon as it is taken from the oven.

This recipe is from the Mother of one of our dearest friends, Jo June Willis Dipboye. She and I were best of friends from the age of ten until her death in 2010.

BANANA POUND CAKE

- 1 c. shortening
- ½ c. butter, softened
- 3 c. sugar
- 5 large eggs
- 3 ripe bananas, mashed
- 3 T. milk
- 2 t. vanilla
- 3 c. flour
- ½ t. salt
- 1 t. baking powder

Beat shortening and butter on medium speed of an electric mixer about 2 minutes until creamy. Gradually add sugar, beating at medium speed 5 to 7 minutes. Add eggs, 1 at a time, beating just until yellow disappears. Combine bananas, milk and vanilla. Combine flour, baking powder and salt. Add banana mixture alternately with flour mixture to shortening mixture, beginning and ending with flour mixture. Beat at low speed just until blended after each addition. Pour batter into a greased and floured 10 inch tube pan. Bake at 350 degrees for 1 hour and 20 minutes or until tooth pick comes out clean. Cool cake in pan on wire rack 10 to 15 minutes; remove from pan and let cool on wire rack.

Glaze: Whipping cream, vanilla and powdered sugar

EXCELSIOR CHEESECAKE

Crust:

Melt ½ c. butter; stir in 2 cups crushed graham crackers. Press into and 2/3 way up the sides of a lightly greased 10 inch spring form pan.

Filling:

Beat 2 lbs. cream cheese, room temperature, until smooth. Add:

- 1 c. sugar
- ½ t. almond extract
- ½ t. vanilla

Batter should have no lumps of cheese. Beat in 2 eggs, but don't over beat at this point. Bake at 350 degrees for 30 to 35 minutes.

Topping:

Whisk together:

- 2 c. sour cream
- ½ t. almond extract
- ¾ c. sugar
- Juice of ½ lemon

Pour on with care; bake 10 minutes more. Chill overnight. This recipe is from Wanda Johns, and the following recipe is from Barbara Joiner. They were very dear

Christian friends, and our families spent many hours together.

ITALIAN CREAM CAKE

Cream:

- 1 stick margarine
- ½ c. shortening
- 2 cups sugar

Add

- 1 tsp. vanilla
- yolks of 5 eggs l at a time

Dissolve 1 t. soda in 1 c. buttermilk and add alternately with 2 c. flour. Add 1 c. coconut and 1 c. chopped pecans. Beat 5 egg whites until stiff and fold into mixture. Bake in three pans at 325 degrees for 35 minutes.

Icing:

1 8 oz. pkg. cream cheese, 1 stick margarine, 1 t. vanilla and 1 box powdered sugar. Beat until creamy. I put the pecans in the frosting instead of the cake.

CAKE THAT DOESN'T LAST

- 3 c. flour
- 2 c. sugar
- 1 t. soda
- 1 t. salt
- 1 t. cinnamon
- 1½ t. vanilla
- 1 c. nuts
- 3 eggs
- 1½ c. oil
- 2 c. mashed bananas
- 1 15 oz. can crushed pineapple with juice

Combine all ingredients by hand until well blended. Pour into a large greased and floured bundt pan. Bake at 350 degrees for 1 hour and 20 minutes.

GHIRADELLI CHOCOLATE CAKE

- 3 c. flour
- 2 c. sugar
- 1 c. Ghiradelli Sweetened Ground Chocolate
- 1 t. salt
- 1 c. buttermilk
- 2 eggs
- 2 t. soda
- 2 t. baking powder
- 1 c. Wesson oil
- 1 t. vanilla
- 1 c. boiling water

Mix in order of recipe all ingredients except boiling water. Mix well and then add boiling water. Bake at 375 degrees for 30 to 35 minutes in 11x 17 inch pan which has been greased and floured. <u>Must use Ghiradelli Sweetened Chocolate.</u>

Icing:

- ½ c. margarine
- ¼ c. milk
- 1 c. Ghiradelli Chocolate
- Pinch salt
- 3 c. sifted powdered sugar
- 1 t. vanilla

In a heavy saucepan, melt butter with milk. Blend in Chocolate and salt. Remove from heat. Add powdered sugar and vanilla. Beat with an electric mixer for 5 minutes or until smooth and glossy.

DONNA'S EASY CHOCOLATE CAKE

Preheat oven to 400 degrees.

In a sauce pan, put 4 T. cocoa, 1 cup water and 2 sticks parkay margarine; bring to a boil while stirring. In a large bowl, mix 2 c. flour and 2 c. sugar then add to above mixture. Stir well and add: 1 t. vanilla, 2 eggs, 1 t. soda and ½ c. buttermilk. Mix well and pour into 11x17 inch pan that has been greased and floured. (Can use Baker's Joy—it's quicker.) Bake for 18 to 20 minutes.

Icing: 1 stick parkay, 6 T. buttermilk and 4 T. cocoa. Bring to boil, stirring constantly; set aside and let cool. When cool, add 1 box powdered sugar and stir.

This recipe is from Donna Hampton, and it makes a delicious cake. Bill and I have been the recipient of the cake from this gracious Christian lady many times. She does so much for so many.

5 MINUTE ALMOND CAKE

- ½ c. butter
- 2 eggs
- 1 c. flour
- 1 c. sugar
- 2 t. almond extract
- 2 T. sliced almonds
- Powdered sugar

Preheat oven to 375 degrees. Melt butter in glass bowl in microwave. Using a fork, beat the eggs into butter. Add the flour, sugar and almond extract and mix well. Pour into an 8 inch cake pan and sprinkle sliced almonds on top. Bake 45 minutes, or until golden brown and a knife inserted near the center comes out clean. Let cool then sprinkle with powdered sugar.

WHITE TEXAS SHEET CAKE

- ½ c, shortening
- 2 c. sugar
- 2 egg whites
- 1 t. salt
- 1 t. soda
- 2 c. flour
- 1¾ c. buttermilk
- 1 t. vanilla

- 1 t. almond flavoring

Frosting:

- 1 stick oleo, melted
- 1 lb. powdered sugar
- 1/3 c. milk
- 1 t. vanilla

Mix shortening, sugar and egg whites together until fluffy, then add soda, salt and flour. Mix together buttermilk, vanilla and almond flavoring and add to the other mixture. Bake in greased and floured 15½x10½ inch pan at 350 degrees for 20 to 25 minutes. Mix together ingredients for frosting and frost cake when cool.

PIES
and PIE CRUSTS

NEVER-FAIL PIE CRUST

- 3 c. all-purpose flour
- 1 t. salt
- 1 c. shortening
- 1 egg
- 1 T. vinegar
- 5 T. water

Combine flour, salt and shortening, cutting until well-mixed. In a separate bowl, beat egg until light. Combine with vinegar and water. Add this to flour- shortening mixture. Knead and roll out as needed. For single crust, bake in 475 degree oven for 8 minutes. Makes 3 single crusts, if you only need one crust, the unused portion can be frozen. Thaw at room temperature before attempting to roll out.

PIE CRUST (1)

- 4 c. flour
- 2 c. Crisco
- 1 t. salt
- 1 c. 7 Up or Sprite, cold

This is from my hair dresser and friend, Lynda Boles, who is a very special person in my life. I am always happier after I visit her.

PIE CRUST (2)

- 3 c. flour
- 1 t. salt
- 1 ½ c. shortening
- 1 medium egg, slightly beaten
- 5 T. ice water
- 1 T. vinegar

Blend flour, salt and shortening. Mix together egg, water and vinegar. Add all at once into flour mix. Makes 2 double pie crusts or 4 baked shells.

This is Bill's pie crust recipe. He is a good cook so this has to be good!

PIE CRUST (3)

- 1 stick butter or oleo
- 1 c. flour
- ½ c. chopped pecans
- ¼ c. powdered sugar

Mix flour, powdered sugar and pecans in pie pan. Pour in melted butter or oleo; press into pie pan with fingers to form crust and bake at 350 degrees until brown. Bake approximately 15 minutes.

APPLE PIE

- 6 c. tart apples, peeled and sliced
- 1 c. sugar
- 1 t. cinnamon
- 2 T. all-purpose flour
- Dash of salt
- ½ t. nutmeg
- 2 T. butter or oleo
- 1 T. lemon juice

If apples lack tartness, sprinkle with lemon juice. Combine sugar, flour, spices and dash of salt. Mix with apples. Line a pie plate with pastry and fill with apples. Dot good over the apples with butter. Sprinkle around the edges of bottom crust to seal the top crust. Cut slits on top crust for steam to escape. Brush the top with milk or cream then sprinkle with sugar. Bake in 400 degree oven for 50 minutes or a little longer if needed.

This is one of my Aunt Louise's recipes, and it makes a delicious pie.

PINEAPPLE CREAM PIE

For pie filling ingredients, you will need:

- 1 large pkg. instant vanilla pudding
- 1 16 oz. carton sour cream
- 1 15¼ oz. can crushed pineapple (undrained)

Mix well and pour into a pie pan filled with the pie crust of your choice, top with cool whip and chill.

KEY LIME PIE (1)

- 4 eggs
- 1 can sweetened condensed milk
- ½ c. key lime juice

Separate eggs; beat yolks slowly with mixer. Add lime juice; slowly blend well. Pour into baked pie shell and top with meringue. Bake at 350 degrees until golden brown.

MERINGUE:

- 4 egg whites
- 1 t. sugar
- ¼ t. vanilla

Beat until stiff and place on top of pie.

KEY LIME PIE (2)

- Chocolate Pie Crust
- 1 can sweetened condensed milk
- ¼ to ½ box powdered sugar
- 1 small can frozen limeade
- 8 oz. carton cool whip

Freeze.

PEACH PINEAPPLE PIE

- 1 can sweetened condensed milk
- 1/3 c. lemon juice
- 1 large carton cool whip

Mix together then fold the following into mixture:

- 1 large can crushed pineapple, drained
- 1 large can sliced peaches, drained

Pour into 2 graham cracker crusts. Chill.

CHERRY O CREAM CHEESE PIE

- 1 crumb crust or 1 baked pastry shell
- 1 8 oz. pkg. cream cheese
- 1 can sweetened condensed milk
- 1/3 c. lemon juice
- 1 t. vanilla
- 1 can cherry pie filling

Soften cream cheese to room temperature and whip until fluffy. Gradually add milk and beat until well blended. Add lemon juice and vanilla. Blend well. Pour into crust and chill 2 to 3 hours before garnishing top of pie with cherry pie filling.

KENTUCKY PECAN PIE

- 1 c. white corn syrup
- 1/3 t. salt
- 1 t. vanilla
- 1 c. dark brown sugar
- 1/3 c. melted butter
- 3 eggs, slightly beaten
- 1 heaping cup shelled whole pecans

Combine syrup, sugar, salt, butter and vanilla and mix well. Add eggs and pour into unbaked pie shell. Sprinkle pecans over top. Bake 350 degrees for 45 minutes.

In the late 1960s, when I was the office manager of an office of 16 women, we took turns bringing dessert for our afternoon break. This pie was brought for a break by a dear lady and friend, Doris Lowery.

PECAN DELIGHT PIE

Beat 3 egg whites, add 1 c. sugar and ¼ t. baking powder. Beat until very stiff. Crush 23 Ritz crackers and add 1 c. pecans; add to egg mixture. Pour into buttered pie pan. Bake at 350 degrees for 25 minutes. Cool completely. Put whipped cream on top and shaved chocolate.

You can use the egg yolks from this pie to make the following chocolate pie:

PUMPKIN PIE

- 1 15 oz. can pumpkin
- 1½ c. brown sugar
- 4 eggs
- 3 T. butter
- 2 T. molasses
- 2 t. cinnamon
- ¾ t. ginger
- ½ t. nutmeg
- 1 t. salt
- 1½ c. milk

Add ingredients to pumpkin in order given. Turn into an unbaked pie shells. Bake in a 425 degree oven for 10 minutes then reduce heat to 325 degrees and bake 30 minutes or until knife inserted in center will come out clean.

STRAWBERRY PIE

Make a pastry shell and cool.

- 1 8 oz. pkg. cream cheese, softened
- 6 T. sour cram
- ½ c. powdered sugar
- 1 to 1½ qts. Strawberries
- 1 c. sugar
- 3 T. corn starch

- Red food coloring

Beat cream cheese until fluffy. Add sour cream and beat until smooth beating in powdered sugar gradually. Spread on bottom of shell and chill. Wash and hull strawberries. Mash enough uneven ones to make 1 cup. Force through a sieve and add water to make one cup. Mix sugar and cornstarch. Add ½ c. water and sieved berries. Cook over medium heat stirring until mixture is thick. Cool and add red food coloring. Fill shell with whole berries tips up and pour sauce over top.

PEANUT BUTTER PIE

- 8 oz. cream cheese, softened and cut into chunks
- 1½ c. powdered sugar
- 1 c. creamy peanut butter
- 1 c. chilled whipping cream
- ½ t. vanilla extract
- 1 ready-made chocolate cookie crumb piecrust

Combine all ingredients, except crust, in the bowl of a food processor and blend until very smooth. An electric mixer on medium speed can be used. Fill crust. Place pie in freezer for at least 2 hours.

Sherry Flint brought this pie to Ladies Bible Class luncheon, and it was delicious!

CHOCOLATE PIE

- 3 egg yolks
- ½ c. sugar
- 3 c. half & half
- 1 pkg. chocolate pudding mix
- 1 c. miniature marshmallows
- 1 t. vanilla

Mix together egg yolks and sugar. Add half & half, pudding mix, marshmallows and vanilla. Cook until thick. Pour into baked pie shell and top with whipped cream.

PERFECT PUMPKIN PIE

- 1 15 oz. can pumpkin
- 1 can sweetened condensed milk
- 2 large eggs
- 1 t. cinnamon
- ½ t. ginger
- ½ t. nutmeg
- ½ t. salt

Heat oven to 425 degrees. Whisk pumpkin, milk, eggs, spices and salt in medium bowl until smooth. Pour into unbaked crust. Bake 15 minutes then reduce oven to 350 degrees; continue baking 35 to 40 minutes or until knife inserted 1 inch from crust comes out clean. Cool.

SKILLET APPLE PIE

- ½ c. unsalted butter
- 1 c. light brown sugar
- 2 refrigerated rolled pie crusts
- 1 21 oz. can apple pie filling
- 2 T. cinnamon sugar

Preheat oven to 400 degrees. Melt the butter in a 9 inch cast iron skillet; set aside 1T. of the melted butter for the top crust. To the melted butter, add the brown sugar and melt them together on medium heat, about 2 minutes. Remove from the heat and line the skillet with one of the pie crusts. Pour the apple pie filling over the crust and sprinkle with 1 T. of the cinnamon sugar. Use the 2nd pie crust to cover the filling. Brush the top with the reserved melted butter, then evenly sprinkle the remaining 1 T. cinnamon sugar on top. Cut vents in the middle of the pie. Bake for 30 minutes. Serve hot with ice cream or the following Cinnamon Whipped Cream: 2 c. whipping cream, 1 t. ground cinnamon and 4 T. sugar.

This recipe is from a dear friend from our Ladies Bible Class, Sharon Childers.

COBBLERS

JIFFY COBBLER

- ½ c. butter
- 1 c. sugar
- 1 c. flour
- 1 c. milk
- 1 t. vanilla
- 1 t. baking powder
- ½ t. salt

Melt butter in a 9x12 inch baking dish. Make a thin batter of remaining ingredients and pour over butter. Pour about 1 quart of sweetened peaches on top of butter. Bake at 375 degrees for 35 minutes. Other fruit can be used instead of peaches.

FRESH BERRY COBBLER

- 4 c. blueberries or sliced strawberries
- 1 c. flour
- ¾ c. sugar
- 2 t. cinnamon
- ½ c. mayonnaise

Place fruit in an 8x8 square baking dish. Stir together next three ingredients; stir in mayonnaise until mixture resembles coarse crumbs. Sprinkle over fruit. Bake at 400 degrees 40 minutes until lightly brown.

CHERRY COBBLER

- 1 can cherries
- 1 c. sugar
- 3 T. flour

Heat cherries in a sauce pan. Mix sugar with flour and add to hot cherries. Heat on low to medium heat until it starts to thicken. Remove from heat and add ½ t. almond flavoring, a small amount of red food coloring and 2 T. butter. Stir and pour into crust. Bake at 425 degrees for 1st 10 minutes and then reduce heat to 400 degrees for approximately 25 minutes.

COOKIES

SNICKERDOODLES

- 3 ¾ c. all-purpose flour
- ½ t. soda
- ½ t. cream of tartar
- ½ t. salt
- 1 c. butter or margarine
- 2 c. sugar
- 2 eggs
- ¼ c. milk
- 1 t. vanilla
- 3 T. sugar
- 1 t. cinnamon

Grease a cookie sheet. Stir together flour, soda, cream of tartar and salt. Beat butter for 30 seconds, add the 2 cups sugar and beat until fluffy. Add eggs, milk and vanilla; beat well. Add dry ingredients to beaten mixture beating until well combined. Form dough into 1 inch balls, roll in a mixture of the 3 T. sugar and 1 t. cinnamon. Place balls 2 inches apart on a cookie sheet and flatten slightly with the bottom of a drinking glass. Bake in a 375 degree oven about 8 minutes or until light golden. Makes about 66 cookies.

This is another one of Bill's "world famous" recipes.

COCONUT COOKIES

- 1 c. sugar
- 1 c. brown sugar
- 1 c. butter
- 3 eggs
- 2½ c. flour
- 1 c. coconut
- 3 c. oatmeal
- 1 t. vanilla
- 1 t. soda
- 1 t. baking powder

Cream sugars and butter. Stir in remaining ingredients. (Will be very hard to stir.) Drop by teaspoon onto greased cookie sheet. Bake at 375 degrees for about 8 minutes. Cookies should be light brown. Do not over bake. Makes about 6 dozen.

This a recipe is from my daddy's cousin's wife, Bertha Playter. Aunt Bertha was my Bible class teacher during my teenage years. From time to time, she would invite our family and the preacher's (J. Ollie Lee) family for a bean supper after evening worship services. The meal consisted of beans, cornbread and cookies. "Happy memories!"

JIFFY PEANUT BUTTER COOKIES

- 1 c. chunk style peanut butter
- ½ c. margarine
- 1 box yellow cake mix
- 2 eggs
- 2 T. water

In a large bowl of electric mixer cut peanut butter and margarine into dry cake mix using low speed of mixer; add eggs and water. Mix well to form dough. Using 1 T. dough for each cookie, shape into balls. Place on ungreased cookie sheet and flatten each cookie with the bottom of glass which has been lightly greased and dipped into sugar. Re-dip the glass for each cookie. For a crisscross effect, flatten each cookie with the floured tines of a fork. Bake in a 350 degree oven for 15 minutes. Makes about 4½ dozen.

NO BAKE CHOCOLATE OATMEAL COOKIES

- 2 c. sugar
- ½ c. milk
- ½ stick oleo
- 3 T. cocoa

Mix and bring to a boil; boil 1 minute. Add 2 c. quick cooking oats, ½ c. chunky peanut butter and 1 t. vanilla.

Stir and drop by spoonful on waxed paper. Dry for 30 minutes.

OATMEAL CRISPIES

- 1 c. shortening
- 1 c. brown sugar
- 1 c. granulated sugar
- 2 eggs, well beaten
- 1 t. vanilla
- 1 t. salt
- 1 t. soda
- 3 c. quick-cooking oatmeal
- ½ c. chopped walnuts
- 1½ c. flour

Thoroughly cream shortening and sugars; add eggs and vanilla and beat well. Add sifted dry ingredients. Add oatmeal and nuts; mix well. Shape in rolls; wrap in waxed paper and chill thoroughly or overnight. Slice ¼ inch thick; bake on ungreased cookie sheet in moderate oven 350 degrees for 10 minutes. Makes 5 dozen.

WHITE CHOCOLATE-ORANGE DREAM COOKIES

- 1 c. butter or margarine, softened
- 2/3 c. firmly packed light brown sugar
- ½ c. granulated sugar
- 1 large egg
- 1 T. grated orange zest
- 2 t. orange extract
- 2¼ c. all-purpose flour
- ¾ t. baking soda
- ½ t. salt
- 1 12 oz. pkg. white chocolate chips

Preheat oven to 350 degrees. In a mixing bowl, beat first 3 ingredients at medium speed of an electric mixer until creamy. Add egg, orange zest and orange extract, beating until blended. Combine flour, baking soda, and salt; gradually add to sugar mixture, beating just until blended after each addition. Stir in chips. Drop dough by rounded table-spoonfuls onto ungreased baking sheets. Bake 10 to 12 minutes; transfer to wire racks to cool completely. Yield: about 3½ dozen cookies.

SOFT LEMONADE COOKIES

- 1 c. butter, softened
- 1 c. sugar
- 2 eggs
- 3 c. all-purpose flour
- 1 t. baking soda
- 1 6 oz. can frozen lemonade concentrate, thawed
- Additional sugar

Heat oven to 400 degrees. In a mixing bowl, cream butter and sugar; add eggs. Combine flour and baking soda; add to the creamed mixture alternately with 1/3 c. of lemonade concentrate. Mix well. Drop by rounded tspfull onto ungreased baking sheets. Bake 7 to 8 minutes. Remove to wire racks. Brush with remaining lemonade concentrate.* Sprinkle with sugar. Cool. Makes 4 to 5 dozen.

*Darcy's secret addition: She adds a "couple of squirts" of lemon juice concentrate to the "remaining lemonade concentrate" then brushes and sprinkles with sugar. Makes them more tart and very moist.

When our friends, Ray and Karen Rayburn, came from Idaho to visit a couple of summers ago, they brought some of these cookies. Their friend, Darcy, had made them for their road trip. They were so good that I asked for the recipe.

LEMON SQUARES

- 1 c. flour
- ¼ c. powdered sugar
- ½ c. butter

Sift flour and sugar into bowl. Blend in butter with "fingertips" until well mixed. Pat unevenly into bottom of 8x8 baking pan. Bake for 20 minutes at 350 degrees. Meanwhile beat together:

- 2 eggs
- 1 c. sugar
- ½ t. baking powder
- 2½ T. fresh lemon juice
- Dash of salt

Pour over baked crust and return to oven for 20 to 25 minutes at same temperature. Cool on rack. Cut into squares and sprinkle with sifted powdered sugar, optional.

This recipe is from Cynthia Regone, the receptionist in the real estate office where I worked for a few years. (I much prefer Accounting to Real Estate!)

PEANUT BUTTER SWIRLS

- ½ c. shortening or margarine
- 1 c. sugar

- 1 egg
- ½ c. peanut butter
- 1 6 oz. pkg. chocolate chips
- 2 T. milk
- 1¼ c. flour
- ½ t. salt
- ½ t. soda

Mix all ingredients except chocolate chips and place dough on wax paper and roll into a rectangle. Melt chocolate chips and spread over dough. Roll up like jelly roll and chill. Slice and bake at 300 degrees for about 7 minutes.

PEANUT BUTTER COOKIES

- 1 large egg, beaten
- 1 c. creamy peanut butter
- 1 c. sugar
- 36 Hershey's Kisses Brand Milk Chocolate

Combine egg, peanut butter and sugar. Mix well. Form into small balls. Place 2 inches apart on greased cookie sheet. Bake in preheated 350 degree oven for 9 minutes. Remove from oven. Place a Chocolate in center of each cookie. Dough will crack. Bake 1 additional minute. Cool on rack. Makes 3 dozen.

PECAN TASSIES

- 1 3 oz. pkg. Cream Cheese
- ½ c. margarine
- 1 c. flour
- Mix together and chill for 2 hours.
- Grease tassie pans lightly and form dough into pans. Pour in Filling:
- 2 eggs, beaten lightly
- 1 c. brown sugar
- 1 t. vanilla
- Dash of salt
- 2/3 c. pecans

Bake at 375 degrees for 20 minutes. Enjoy!

Note: A tassie pan is a mini cupcake pan.

CANDY

MARTHA WASHINGTON CHOCOLATE BALLS

Filling:

- 1½ boxes powdered sugar (24 oz.)
- 1 c. coconut
- 1 stick of butter, melted
- 2 c. pecans, chopped
- 1 can sweetened condensed milk

Mix all together and let chill for 2 hours.

Melt together in a double boiler:

- 12 oz. pkg. chocolate chips
- 2 oz. stick of paraffin

Roll filling into balls and then roll in the melted chocolate chips. Place on wax paper and let set for about 30 minutes.

ORANGE COCONUT BALLS

- 2¾ c. crushed vanilla wafers
- 1 c. powdered sugar
- ¼ c. frozen orange juice concentrate
- ¼ c. butter, melted
- 1 c. pecans, finely chopped

Mix well and form into balls. Mixture will be crumbly. Set aside for 20 minutes.

Mix:

- 2 c. powdered sugar
- 2 T. butter, melted
- 1 t. vanilla
- Pinch of salt

Add enough milk for spreading. Roll balls in above mixture then in Angel Flake coconut. Let set until dry and not sticky.

EASY DO CHOCOLATE PEANUT CLUSTERS

- 1 24 oz. pkg. chocolate almond bark
- 1 16 oz. jar dry roasted peanuts
- 1 dollop smooth peanut butter (approx. ½ c.)

Put almond bark in a large microwavable bowl. Micro wave for 90 to 120 seconds, depending on your microwave. Stir in peanut butter until it melts in the melted chocolate. Add peanuts and stir until peanuts are covered. Spoon on to wax paper and let set up. (About 10 to 15 minutes) You can leave out the peanut butter, but it is smoother with the peanut butter.

PEANUT BRITTLE

- 3 c. sugar
- 1 c. white Karo syrup
- ½ c. water
- 1½ c. raw peanuts
- 3 T. butter
- 1 t. salt
- 2 t. soda

Boil sugar, syrup and water until syrup spins a thread. It will take a while so be sure it spins a thread on a spoon. Add peanuts and stir continuously. Cook until the mixture turns dark golden brown. You must stir as peanuts will burn if you don't. Remove from heat, stir in butter, salt and soda. Pour into buttered pan; chill and break. Do not spread brittle out with spoon after it is poured out in pans. It will make it tough. It needs the bubble to be tender.

AUNT BILL'S CANDY

- 2 c. sugar
- 1 c. buttermilk
- 1 t. soda (stir into buttermilk)
- 1 stick of butter
- 1 c. pecans

Cook to soft ball stage. Remove from heat and start beating. Beat until it is no longer shiny. Last add the nuts and drop by spoonful onto waxed paper or pour into buttered pan. You must use butter for this recipe.

MARSHMALLOW TREATS

- ¼ c. margarine or butter
- 6 to 10 oz. (about 40) regular marshmallows or 4 c. miniature marshmallows
- 5 c. Rice Krispy's

Melt margarine in a saucepan. Add marshmallows and cook over low heat, stirring constantly until marshmallows are melted and mixture is very syrupy. Remove from heat. Add Rice Krispy's cereal and stir until well coated. Press warm mixture evenly and firmly into a buttered 13x9x2 inch pan. Cut into squares when cool. Yield: 24 2x2 inch squares. Note: About 2 c. marshmallow crème may be substituted for marshmallows. Add to melted margarine and cook over low heat about 5 minutes, stirring constantly. Proceed as above.

BREADS

VEAH'S NO KNEAD ROLLS

- 2 c. warm water
- 2 t. salt
- 2 pkg. yeast
- ¼ c shortening
- ½ c. sugar
- 1 egg
- 6½ c. flour

Mix well. Do not knead. Let rise until double. Make into rolls and let rise. Bake at 400 degrees for 20 to 30 minutes. Can be stored covered in the refrigerator when doubled. It will keep 4 or 5 days.

This recipe is from the grandmother of my favorite son-in- law, David Perkins.

CRESCENT ROLLS

- 2 T. sugar
- 6 T. shortening
- 1 t. salt

Mix and stir in:

- 1½ c. lukewarm milk
- 2 pkgs. Yeast

Stir until dissolved and add:

- 4 c. sifted flour

Beat. Scrape dough from sides of bowl and cover bowl with damp cloth. Let rise until double—about 30 minutes. Roll out dough, cut and shape into crescents. Cover. Let rise 15 minutes. Bake until golden brown about 12 to 15 minutes at 425 degrees. Makes 2 dozen.

SOUR CREAM ROLLS

- 2¾ c. all-purpose flour
- 2 T. sugar
- 1 pkg. rapid rise yeast
- 1 t. salt
- ¾ c. sour cream
- ¼ c. water
- 2 T. butter or margarine
- 1 egg

Combine 1 cup of flour, sugar, dry yeast and salt in a large mixer bowl. Heat sour cream, water and butter until very warm. Add to flour mixture. Beat 2 minutes at medium speed. Add egg and remaining 1¼ c. flour to make a soft batter. Spoon evenly into 12 greased muffin cups. Cover, let rise until doubled in size, about 1 hour. Bake at 400 degrees for 15 to 18 minutes or until golden brown. Remove from pans; cool on wire rack.

EASY HOT ROLLS

- 1 pkg. yeast
- ¼ c. warm water
- 2 T. sugar

Mix and let stand for 15 minutes and add:

- 1 egg
- 1 c. warm water
- ½ c. sugar
- ½ t. salt
- ¼ c. Crisco oil
- 4 c. self-rising flour.

Let rise and shape into rolls. Let rise again and bake at 375 degrees until golden brown.

NEVER FAIL ROLLS

- 2 c. lukewarm water
- 1 pkg. yeast
- 1 T. salt
- ¾ c. sugar
- 2 eggs, slightly beaten
- ½ c. Crisco, melted and warm
- 6 c. flour

Mix in order; let rise until double. Refrigerate in air tight container overnight. Bake at 350 degrees until golden brown.

REFRIGERATOR ROLLS

- 1 pkg. instant potatoes (4 servings)
- 4 ½ c. to 4 ¾ c. flour
- 1 pkg. dry yeast
- ½ c. shortening
- ½ c. sugar
- 1 c. milk
- 2 eggs
- 1 t. salt

Prepare potatoes as directed. Add yeast to 2 c. flour. In a sauce pan, heat milk, shortening, sugar and salt until warm. Stir in potatoes then add to flour mixture; add eggs. Beat at low speed for 1 minute and high for 3 minutes. Add rest of flour. Store in refrigerator until needed.

PATTY'S CORN BREAD

- 1 c. self-rising corn meal
- 2 eggs
- 1 c. milk
- ¼ c. Wesson oil
- 1 can cream style corn
- 1 lb. bacon, fried and crumbled
- ½ lb. ground beef, browned
- 1 or 2 sausage patties, fried and crumbled (opt.)
- 1 large onion, chopped
- 2 c. cheddar cheese, divided
- ½ c. jalapeno peppers, buy chopped and chop finer
- 2 T. sour cream (opt.)

Mix in order given using ½ cheese in casserole and other ½ on top. Oil a large casserole and sprinkle with corn meal. Bake at 425 degrees for 45 minutes.

MEXICAN CORN BREAD

- 1 T. baking powder
- 1 c. yellow corn meal
- 1½ t. salt
- 2 eggs
- 1 c. sour cream
- 1 c. oil
- 1 c. cream style corn

- 2 jalapeno peppers, chopped
- ½ c. grated cheese

Mix all ingredients except cheese and pour into lightly greased pan. Top with cheese. (I put the cheese in the mixture before baking.) Bake for 1 hour at 350 degrees.

This recipe is from my favorite son, John. (He is my only son!)

MISCELLANEOUS

CORN BREAD DRESSING

- 1½ c. finely chopped onion
- 1½ c. finely chopped celery
- 1/3 c. butter or margarine
- 8 c. crumbled corn bread
- 1½ t. salt
- 1/8 t. pepper
- ½ t. poultry seasoning
- ½ t. ground sage
- ¼ c. water
- 1 egg, well beaten

Cook onion and celery until tender in melted butter in a large Dutch oven. Add crumbled corn bread. Sprinkle with seasonings. Add water and egg; toss together and mix well. Stuff turkey or place in a greased 4 quart casserole and bake at 325 degrees for 25 minutes or until lightly browned.

SLOW COOKER DRESSING

- 4 eggs, slightly beaten
- 2/3 c. celery, chopped
- 2/3 c. onion, chopped
- 3 T. rubbed sage
- Salt & Pepper to taste

- 2 14.5 oz. cans chicken broth
- 1 can cream of chicken soup
- 1 8 inch square pan of corn bread, cooked and crumbled
- 8 to 10 slices bread, toasted and crumbled

Mix all ingredients together and pour into greased slow cooker. Cook on high 3 to 3½ hours. If you want to fix chicken and dressing, boil chicken breasts and add to mixture.

POPCORN BALLS

- 1 c. water
- ½ c. Griffin white syrup
- 2 c. sugar
- 1 t. salt
- 1 t. vanilla
- 2 t. vinegar

Bring to hard boil stage, and pour over popped corn. Stir to coat well and shape into balls.

This is another recipe from Donna Hampton. I have never made these, but we have been the recipient of these popcorn balls from Donna. She uses 6 bags of microwave Home Style Pop Secret Popcorn. They are so delicious!

STRAWBERRY PRESERVES

- 1 qt. berries, cleaned and washed
- 3 T. pure apple cider vinegar

Bring to boil and add

- 4 c. sugar

Boil hard 6 to 8 minutes.

SPICED PRUNES

- 1 lb. dried prunes
- ½ c. vinegar
- 1 2 inch stick cinnamon
- ½ t. whole allspice
- 1¼ c. sugar
- ½ c. pineapple juice
- 1 t. whole cloves

Place prunes in a jar or crock. Combine pineapple juice, vinegar, sugar, cinnamon, cloves and allspice. Bring to a boil and simmer 5 minutes. Pour over prunes. Cover and let stand 3 days in refrigerator before using.

HOT CRANBERRY PUNCH

- 1 tea bag
- 1 c. boiling water

- 1 c. cranberry juice cocktail
- 3 c. apple cider or unsweetened apple juice
- 1 cinnamon stick, cracked
- 4 whole cloves
- 4 allspice berries
- 1 strip orange peel, about 2 inches long and ½ inch wide
- 4 thin orange slices, opt.
- 4 cinnamon sticks, opt.

Place the tea bag in a mug, add the boiling water, steep for 5 minutes and remove the tea bag. In a saucepan, combine the cranberry juice cocktail, apple cider, cinnamon stick, cloves, allspice and orange peel and bring to a boil over a medium heat. Reduce heat, cover and simmer for 15 minutes. Remove saucepan from heat and add the prepared tea to the saucepan.

Strain the punch into 4 mugs and garnish each drink with an orange slice and cinnamon stick.

TIPSY FRUIT

- Fresh fruit in season (melons, berries, grapes etc.)
- 1 c. triple sec
- 1/3 c. powdered sugar

Put cubed fruit into hollowed out watermelon half. Mix triple sec and powdered sugar and pour over fruit. Let marinate.

BLUEBERRY BLAST SMOOTHIE

- 1 c. blueberries, fresh or frozen
- 1 banana, peeled
- ½ c. nonfat plain yogurt
- ½ c. fresh orange juice
- 4 to 5 ice cubes
- 1 T. fresh lemon juice
- 1 T. fresh mint leaves, chopped
- Whole leaves for garnish, opt.

Combine blue berries, banana, yogurt, orange juice, ice cubes, lemon juice and mint in blender jar. Blend until smooth, about 2 minutes. Pour into glasses and serve immediately.

GOOD SCENTS POTPOURRI

- 1 apple, quartered
- 1 cinnamon stick, broken
- 1 t. whole cloves
- 2 dashes nutmeg
- ½ sliced orange

In saucepan, cover spices and fruit with water and warm over low heat. Add water as needed. This makes your house smell really good.

Made in the USA
San Bernardino, CA
01 July 2015